TEACH NEW DOGS OLD TRICKS

MASTERING NEW MARKETING TECHNOLOGY WITH OLD MARKETING WISDOM

MATT BAILEY

LEADERS IN GLOBAL PUBLISHING

Published by Motivational Press, Inc.
1777 Aurora Road
Melbourne, Florida, 32935
www.MotivationalPress.com

Manufactured in the United States of America.

ISBN: 978-1-62865-374-8

Contents

FORWARD

My Sales Journey

AFTER I GRADUATED HIGH SCHOOL, I needed a way to pay for college. My grades weren't going to do it, and my chances for an athletic scholarship disappeared with an injury. I enlisted and served in the Army National Guard and trained as a medic.

After returning home from my training, classes didn't start for another 4 months, so I needed a job. That's when my father advised sales training.

I did not have a good impression of salesmen (as we called them back then). They seemed slick and oily, and were always portrayed negatively on TV. What came to mind was Herb Tarlick from *WKRP in Cincinnati*, a show I watched as a kid in the 70s and 80s. Herb was willing to say or do anything to get the deal, or willing to work two hours to get out of an hour of work. That is what was in my head.

Sales training? It just seemed …. "icky." The image in my mind wasn't positive.

Then my dad showed me a library of sales books, training tapes, and guides. He had been through sales training many years ago. He was a pastor, and I wondered why he needed sales training. He told me that sales training taught him many things that he still used in the pulpit of his church.

What he taught me was that sales was about people. You need to genuinely get to know them and their needs. Sometimes, you can match a solution to their need, and sometimes, you can't. But the point of getting to know people was to build lifetime relationships. Someday maybe you can help them. He showed me how those lifetime relationships build a network of influence which far outreaches the initial idea of "sales."

Then he even offered to help pay for it. (In reality, that's what made my decision.)

He was right. I learned invaluable lessons about how people think, how they are persuaded, how we interpret information, and how our perceptions can change everything. Sales wasn't about "getting the sale." It was a guide for better communication, gaining insight, and learning more about people.

It wasn't long before I started working with the new technology of the Internet. I started building websites and learning how the Internet worked in 1995. Eventually I built a website to sell commercial real estate properties and businesses. That sales training experience came to be immensely helpful. The website was my new sales tool, and it had to reflect that purpose.

> SALES TRAINING HELPS YOU BUILD LIFETIME RELATIONSHIPS THAT CREATE A NETWORK OF INFLUENCE WHICH FAR EXCEEDS THE INITIAL IDEA OF "SALES."

Fast forward a few decades.... Now we have a generation of website builders, marketing directors, and consultants who know about the tactics of marketing online but do not understand the underlying principles of what drives everything. *Sales. People. Relationships.*

Technology to today's digital marketers is second nature, but most have never learned the principles of persuasion, or the tried-and-true sales techniques that enable better communication and lead generation.

I've found that sales skills aren't obsolete. They are needed now more than ever. This book is written to those of you who need to retrofit those seemingly "rusty" skills into the shiny new space, or to learn new-old techniques that will transform your online marketing capabilities and take them to the next level.

Establish Rapport

Analyze Searcher Behavior

O NE OF THE FIRST THINGS that I learned in sales training was to establish rapport. You need to find common ground - something you share to establish the beginning of the relationship.

This has been overdone in too many instances. When done incorrectly or insincerely, it seems creepy, and can be overbearing.

Starting the Relationship

What makes building rapport such a fine-tuned activity is one little discipline. That discipline is approaching people with genuine interest in them and not false friendship. As the salesperson, my job is to find something in common with you. It is NOT to help you find something in common with me. Too many sales people turned this into a game where they could find one little item and make it about themselves - if that happens, they've lost. No potential customer wants to hear a salesperson blather on about themselves.

No, this is all about the customer. It tales work and experience to make it as subtle as possible. It takes a skill of drawing out information from a prospect without being overbearing, but being sensitive enough to know when to ask for more information or when to change the line of questioning. It also takes a second conversation in your own mind - processing what you've heard.

The key is listening to the prospect's answers, as therein lie the real problems. But let's leave listening to another chapter.

YOU'VE GOT WHAT I WANT

Online, establishing rapport is much simpler than a live conversation with another person in a sales situation. However, it takes similar listening and creative thinking skills to be able to deduce the next steps in the process.

What makes the online rapport process easier is that people are much more comfortable going online for information, rather than picking up the phone and talking to a salesperson. Right? This is what Google calls "MicroMoments," the moment that inspiration becomes action - and people search for ideas and answers.

Searching for information online has become the default mode of asking questions. No hassle, no commitments - people just find the information they need. They can dream about a vacation without talking to a travel agent, research a new car without going to the dealer, compare appliances before going to the store, or investigate options without talking to a salesperson.

People search constantly. It's an activity that does not show any signs of slowing down. People search for anything, from mundane trivia to life-threatening disease treatments. It's been built into our nature in just a few short decades.

Now, when you search using a search engine, you are immediately faced with the establishment of rapport, even without you knowing it.

Search results pages from Bing (left) and Google (right)

You may have noticed it before, but in these search results, the terms that you type into the search box are repeated throughout the results and bolded. This is a very simple function, but it does amazing things for your brain. You do not have to look at the results word for word. Your brain recognizes the pattern and the words that you typed into the box. At this point, your brain and eyes are simply scanning the page for large bold-color blocks.

Results that have more of your words will have more bolded text in the results. Searchers tend to click the results that have more bolded terms in them, even without much "reading," because they immediately show more relevance. The more words that match means that the more this page must answer my need. Right?

Now the key is that your website must match the phrase and intent of the searcher in both the "snippet" of results, and in the entirety of the page it represents. The searcher is on a quest for information, and *you must deliver that answer*. You must know the words that people use to search, and predict the accompanying information that is critical to their decision-making.

Without this information, or the execution of it in your marketing, visitors will leave without finding their information, and will become one of the 90% of visitors that see your website, leave, and never come back again.

So, what do searchers want? This comes down to your preparation for the sales call. We used to call this the **Pre-Call Research**. This is researching everything you could about a prospect before the call, so that you could anticipate questions, be prepared for objections, and be able to build rapport effectively. Online, we need to know the words, and intent behind those words, to have an effective "sales call," or website visit.

Fortunately, research into the prospect's mind is available to us. Unfiltered by focus groups or polls, this research is the most direct way to tap into the minds and motivations of searchers. Keyword Research enables you to find the language and words that connect you with the searcher.

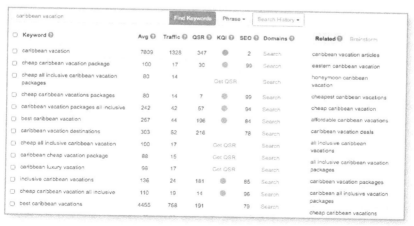

Keyword research from Jaaxy.com

In this simple report, we can learn a lot from the data about searchers and their intent. This takes the top searches with the words "caribbean vacation" and shows you many of the variations used by searchers.

By examining the words people use in their searches, you can develop a potential profile of that searcher and their expectations. When you go through the words, you can group them, to learn more about different searchers and what is important to them:

- **Budget Factors:** cheap, cheapest, all inclusive, deals, luxury, affordable
- **Rating Factors:** best, top, best value
- **Types:** beach, secluded, resort, rentals, honeymoon
- **Word Choice:** book, package, destination, getaway, travel
- **Research:** articles, comparison, ideas

As you can see, there is far more nuance to this phrase, "caribbean vacation," than meets the eye. We have to deal with different word choices, intents, budgets, and destination ideas. Attempting to sell someone on a Caribbean vacation without knowing any of the particulars presents a very general approach, which is rarely effective.

Our chances of making a better connection or building better rapport improve if I can get some additional detail from the searcher, and send them to a page about that particular item. If someone is searching for *'best caribbean vacation deals,'* they most likely will not respond to the same offer as someone searching for a *'luxury vacation package.'*

As a competent salesperson, I would adjust my sales pitch, based on knowing this information. The same happens online when search engines match searchers to the most relevant page. The better you present particular relevant information, rather than attempting to be a catch-all to any inquiry, the more effective you are in reaching and retaining the interest of the searcher.

This comes down to understanding the words that searchers use, and using them in your sales presentation on the pages of your website. In sales, this technique is called **Mirroring**.

MIRRORING

USING THE CUSTOMER'S WORDS TO UNDERSTAND NEEDS

IN SIMPLE TERMS, THE MIRRORING or Reflecting sales technique listens for key words and concepts expressed by the customer, and then uses those words in their conversation.

This is why Search Engine Optimization is such a critical component of online marketing. Using the right words enables your website to be found in the right search results. Ignorance of the customer's words, descriptions, and searched problems will limit your company's visibility in search results.

Search engines can account for more than 70 - 80% of a website's visitors. If your site does not use the same words the customer uses, they will never find you. This is easier than you might imagine, but it takes work to get out of the "internal jargon" mindset.

Let's dig a little deeper into the principles that are found in this technique and see how they can work for you.

THE MIRRORING PRINCIPLE

In mirroring, the salesperson listens for word cues expressed by the potential customer. This is called **Active Listening**. There are two specific cues that are critical: the customer's communication type and expressed needs.

COMMUNICATION TYPE

The words used by a person express his or her psychological approach. For example, if the customer focuses on the visual, he will say phrases like, "I see." If a customer is more auditory, she will say phrases like, "That sounds good." If more cognitive, you will hear phrases like, "I get it," or "I understand."

A trained salesperson hears these auditory cues and reflects his language to mirror the expressed preference of communication - visual, auditory, or cognitive. If the customer is more visual, the salesperson will change their presentation to say things like, "How does this look to you?" Additionally, the salesperson will use phrases like, "Look here," or "As we can see." This is the first part of Mirroring.

EXPRESSED NEEDS

The second part of this classic sales technique is to listen for expressed problems or issues, and respond by using the same words to ask questions, present alternatives, or delve into deeper issues. While this does take some mastery, the effect is impactful to a customer.

The customer feels that the salesperson is truly listening to them and understands them. The trust level increases dramatically. When we feel that the salesperson knows and understands us, we are at ease. Because they use our words, it shows that they have listened, and understand the situation. All they have been doing is listening and using our words and phrases as they speak back to us. But what we hear is familiarity. It puts the customer at ease, and makes them more open.

This is certainly not to say that the technique fools us, or that the salesperson is simply repeating words. This technique causes a deeper level of empathy in salespeople, and is especially effective when the salesperson is focused on building a relationship, not just a sale.

Now, let's look at how the mirroring principle translates into using keywords online.

THE KEYWORD PRINCIPLE

Keywords are our ability to mirror online. By knowing the words that customers use and reflecting those words in our websites and online marketing content, we show that we understand their questions and needs.

Unfortunately, Search Engine Optimization (SEO) has developed a reputation of "behind the scenes" black magic and countless unsavory tactics. Too many companies have bad stories and negative experiences of working with an SEO company.

Despite the reputation, this is the heart of what SEO is all about: learning and implementing the words of the potential customer into your marketing, so that, when they search on a subject, you increase your ability to be found. It's as simple as that. Everything else is built on that foundation.

While search engine optimization can get complicated very quickly, the basics are necessary to have your website compete in the search results. It all starts with keywords.

In-depth keyword research not only informs you as to which words customers use to search, but it also provides insights as to how those words and concepts are used. Context is the key. Rather than just looking at a list of keywords that is generated from the research, take the time to group, examine, analyze, and find commonalities among the phrases.

Remember, this is pure customer-based market research. Keywords are the direct link to the mind of the customer/searcher. This is where they tell you what they want.

Look at groups of words by phrase, location, brand name, concern, and association. Searchers are telling you what they want to find. They are telling you information beyond just the primary word. They are providing the context of multiple words, concepts, and related information that is important to their buying behavior and research.

KEYWORD MARKET RESEARCH EXAMPLE: HIKING

In this example, I am showing a keyword research report from Jaaxy.com. As with most keyword research websites, you type in a word or phrase and the results will show you how people search that term, and the associated terms and phrases they use.

Typically, the report will show an estimated number of searches in a specific time period. From this, you can gather the popularity of certain phrases. But by no means are these numbers completely accurate or exhaustive. They are primarily extrapolated reports from small data points published by the search engines.

From a market research perspective, I recommend learning the associations, groupings, and inquiries expressed by searchers. This enables me to find specific questions or interests that could be added into my content marketing strategy.

For the keyword "hiking," you can start to develop specific types of searches and needs based on the associated keywords. Products, locations, types of hiking, and associated brands provide greater insight into the market.

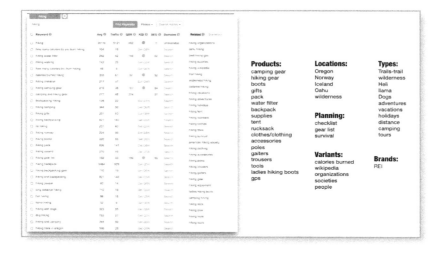

Products:
camping gear
hiking gear
boots
gifts
pack
water filter
backpack
supplies
tent
rucksack
clothes/clothing
accessories
poles
gaiters
trousers
tools
ladies hiking boots
gps

Locations:
Oregon
Norway
Iceland
Oahu
wilderness

Planning:
checklist
gear list
survival

Variants:
calories burned
wikipedia
organizations
societies
people

Types:
Trails-trail
wilderness
Heli
llama
Dogs
adventures
vacations
holidays
distance
camping
tours

Brands:
REI

BUILD CREDIBILITY

LOOK PROFESSIONAL, ONLINE AND OFFLINE

CREDIBILITY IS CRUCIAL TO GAINING a prospective customer's trust. In my college years, I learned some valuable lessons about credibility when I was introduced to Aristotle's Rhetoric. As it was written around the 4th Century BC, it is one of the earliest works to analyze the elements of persuasion. I was immediately drawn to this work because it contained so many of the sales principles that I had learned, and they had been laid out clearly, over 2,000 years ago.

According to Aristotle, there are three elements of persuasion: logic, emotion, and credibility.

Logic is the strength of your argument.

Emotion is the drive of the individual that is listening, and is the primary decision-making factor.

Credibility is the trust that the speaker is knowledgeable, and has the interest of their audience at heart.

How can we test and use this information today? Let's look at how these elements work for online applications.

BUILD CREDIBILITY IN THE ONLINE MARKETPLACE

One of the earliest studies on credibility and websites was performed by the Stanford Persuasive Technology Lab. The researchers tested numerous websites to find out what made one website more credible than another. The results were really not that astonishing, but clarified an important point.

Test subjects associated visual appeal with credibility. But visual appeal did not always mean an emphasis on the design or imagery. No, the subjects noted particular elements as contributing to their overall credibility judgments:

1. Typography
2. Layout
3. Font Size
4. Color Scheme

It was less about the imagery and more about the readability of a website that resulted in being judged as credible. It was more than just the words. The organization and hierarchy of the information on the page was important. People trusted a highly structured presentation of the content.

This means that the test subjects preferred pages with clear headings, readability of the font size, a layout that was conducive to the content, and a color scheme that was highly contrasted for easy reading. These elements help to focus a website visitor on the information on the page, the importance of the primary elements, and the readability of the information. This is what they assessed as "visual appeal."

As marketing moves to mobile and app interfaces, this becomes an even more critical need. Content needs to be primarily readable with clear, understandable labels and information hierarchy. The colors should complement the text and layout of the content, and not hide it. Smaller screens will require more attention to these details, or they will simply be rejected by users.

CREATE CREDIBILITY

There is an additional factor in these elements that determine credibility. It is that online users simply browse pages. Depending upon which studies you read, eight seconds is about the average time that a person will spend looking at and evaluating your webpage.

What can someone view in eight seconds?

- Headlines
- Subheadings
- Images
- Callouts
- Linked text
- Bolded text
- Bullet Points

Mere seconds are not a long time to assess a webpage. However, if you know that you have a limited time to get your message across—and that people's eyes will skip around the pages, pausing at these elements to determine relevance—you can use these elements to your advantage.

You can implement the primary words, content, and phrases from your research to create an organized, contextual presentation on the page. When the visitor's eyes are roaming about the page, they will see the keyword phrases that suit the content being used in these important page elements, and you can persuade them to stay longer and do more. Not only have you made a more credible presentation, you have presented relevant content in primary page areas, and may have answered their question.

BREAKING DOWN THE FACTORS

Three of the main factors are typography, layout, and font size. All of them surround a hierarchy of the content as it is presented to the reader. Based on the size of the text, typography used, and layout, you can deduce that it is a headline. It is the largest text on the page.

Subheadings are identifiable because they are larger than regular text. They have more size and weight, signifying that they are more important than the text, but less important than the main heading.

Smaller headings will be larger than the text, but provide sub-points that direct visitor attention to appropriate content blocks. By utilizing clear word labels that introduce the content, a reader can scan the page quickly, checking off multiple headings, until they see the word or words that are specific to their query.

As you can surmise, this is a basic outline of the hierarchy of content.

Headline - Title

1. Subheading 1

    a. Sub-point

    b. Sub-point

2. Subheading 2

    a. Sub-point

    b. Sub-point

3. Subheading 3

    a. Sub-point

    b. Sub-point

You probably recognize this. It's a basic skeleton for organizing a content outline. You may have had to do this in high school. It's taught and used because it works. It helps you develop your thinking into an organized format. By developing your content in a topical hierarchy of importance and identifying the details under each subheading, your page practically formats itself.

TEXT SIZE

The credibility factor of text size is one that does not get enough attention. From my years testing websites, I've heard a common complaint among test subjects: that too many websites use small fonts, too small for easy reading. Many users do not know that they can increase the size of the text in the browser. You cannot rely on the end user to know many browser functions.

The funny thing about text size is that we are conditioned not to trust small text. From a sales standpoint, it is a well-known joke that you can't trust "the fine print." We are taught not to trust big paragraphs of small text that are difficult to read. What do you usually see on webpages? You see big paragraphs of small text that no one wants to read.

For a client's website, I ran an interesting test. The target audience was an age range of 50-70 years of age. Simply by increasing the text size, we increased the conversion rate by 15%. This may not be the rule for all sites, but keep in mind that while people may not read every word on your website, they want to know that they CAN read every word. It would be even better if they could read those words without eye strain.

COLOR SCHEME

When it comes to eye strain, nothing will do it faster than a lack of contrast between the text and the background. Reading on an electronic device provides a significant hindrance when compared to reading words on a printed page. Electronic screens, while still improving, do not offer significant levels of contrast, as compared to printed versions. Therefore, eye fatigue sets in faster, and distractibility is increased.

Poor contrast hinders reading, and many people will simply not see low-contrast elements on the page. Naturally, they will skip over those areas. Eye testing studies show us that online users will always look at high-contrast areas on the page, and they will ignore low-contrast areas.

This is why my rule in presenting a call to action is that it needs to be **the biggest, boldest, highest contrast element on the page**. It needs to be visible, and high contrast makes it visible. The most contrast you can provide online is black text on a white background. This is why every book you read has black text on a white page. It's the easiest on the eyes to read and does not present a fatigue factor.

In this example, both sites are selling the same services, yet one site is perceived to be more credible than the other. The website on the left has a clear content hierarchy. There are clear headings, subheadings, and calls to action. The snippets of text are easy to read because of the white space surrounding them, giving the eye an easy target to scan.

The website on the right uses the same font size throughout the presentation, but changes the color and contrast by switching headings to white text on a color background. This has the effect of minimizing the importance of the headings, as a simple color change is not enough. The text presented in each area does not have enough white space to provide easy reading. The text appears condensed and heavy, and does not invite scanning to find information.

CREDIBILITY CHECK-UP

How can you build a visitor's trust online? **Make a clear presentation of your content**.

Basically, approach the design of your website and pages from the point of view of customers who are barely paying attention, because *they are* barely paying attention.

LISTEN MORE THAN TALK

GET MORE DATA TO SOLVE THE PROBLEM

O NE OF THE MOST DIFFICULT concepts to grasp in sales training is listening. I remember one of the students in the sales training class having an extreme reaction to being told that he talked too much and didn't listen enough.

"How will they know what I do if I don't tell them?" he exclaimed. That question defined the problem, according to the instructor. "How will you know what they need if you don't hear?" he calmly replied.

The value of listening is so great that there is an unspoken rule in sales: **He who talks the most, loses**.

This applies in so many areas: job interviews, client meetings, sales presentations, the sales floor, and trade shows. If you are doing most of the talking, you are not making the sale. It is a great measurement as to how well you are doing by how much the prospect talks.

The problem is that we think we are offering a persuasive pitch. If the customer does not respond, we restate and re-approach the subject from another angle. All the while, we are ignorant of the true needs of the customer. The less the prospect/customer talks, the less you know about them, and the less chance you have of converting them.

MORE INFORMATION PROVIDES MORE OPPORTUNITY

It's a simple equation. The more you, as the salesperson, listen, the more information you have at your disposal, so you can ask more relevant questions. Then you can introduce the customer to a solution. The best salespeople allow the customers to sell themselves. They only guide the conversation, they don't dominate it.

If you feel that the customer is ignorant, and it is up to you to inform and persuade them, then you will not have much success. The customer invariably walks away, thinking that you do not know anything about them.

Success in sales is built on trust. Trust is built by listening and showing concern. True listening skills allow for more information, more openings, and more matches to the customer needs, which are only expressed by the customer.

This is difficult, as it tends to depart from common sense; we have to talk and tell our story, right?

In my own experience, there are two areas where I've seen this strategy work wonders. First, in job interviews. Job interviews are always nerve-racking events. However, after sales training, they became much more enjoyable, sometimes even fun. The game of "who talks the most" is in play.

In the interviews where I did the least amount of talking, they were noticeably better, more relaxed experiences. In one interview, they offered me another job at a higher level, with a better salary. Because that interviewer did most of the talking, he brought up another position in the conversation, which ended up being a better fit for the company and for me.

Secondly, I see this play out in my current position as a consultant. The best training sessions and meetings are the ones in which the clients take over and talk about their strategy. Once they get to that point, I simply guide the conversation.

What I've realized is that most companies have not had this kind of sharing and communication. When their company data is on the table, and they learn the established principles of marketing or analysis, they have a basis to form a strategy. The worst thing I can do is take that away by talking more and eliminating the conversation.

LISTENING = GATHERING DATA

Let's apply this to Digital Marketing. You need to gather as much information about the customer as possible. Then respond by presenting offers and information that correspond to the expressed needs of the customer.

If you are like me, you get an astounding amount of Emails each day. Most of the Emails do not receive more than a few seconds of attention, mainly because of three primary elements: they are not personal, relevant, or timely.

It quickly becomes obvious which retailers are using purchasing data (at the least) and maybe browsing data to inform their campaigns. Those are the ones that are delivering interesting and attractive Emails throughout the year. Without using this data, the same message is being delivered to everybody. Unfortunately, when sending the same message to everybody, that usually means it is relevant to nobody.

Trying to send the same message to tens of thousands of recipients does not take into account the unique needs, preferences, and history of each customer. By taking simple steps to segment your audience, you can deliver relevant messages that will increase the interest of the intended audience.

This became painfully obvious when I was searching for an automotive part online. One of my hobbies is working on an old 1964 Volkswagen Beetle. While driving around one day, my brakes felt "mushy." In moments I didn't have any brakes at all. Fortunately I got the car into a parking lot and towed it home. After getting underneath the car to find the problem, it all came down to a $5 part that had failed, and all of my brake fluid leaked out of the system.

I went online to find the part at numerous retailers. For some reason, it was out of stock at most of the retailers that I tend to use, so I did not purchase the part right away.

In the days that followed, one retailer sent me three Emails, which focused on getting my car ready for summer with wax and shine deals. The second Email was themed around restoration with a picture of a Chevy truck. It wasn't even about Volkswagen Beetles. The third Email was themed on tune-up specials and featured pictures of motorcycles, cars, and trucks. I did not receive one Email from the retailer where I had a history of purchasing Volkswagen parts! It was like a salesperson trying to sell me something that was irrelevant, because <u>they did not listen to my problem</u>.

Another retailer did not have the part in stock, so I asked to be notified when the part was available. Very soon after I received an Email about VW Beetle brakes. Interestingly, the Email was an offer to replace and upgrade my entire brake system, which would cost about $500. As a bonus, for that week only, I could get it for 10% off, and with free shipping! They earned my business and respect.

Personal

Relevant

Timely

No Email is interesting to me, unless it meets my immediate or near-future need. Knowing your customers is only possible by investing in the right technology that enables you to make better offers to the right person at the right time.

Responding to your customers' browsing histories on your website, or their past purchase histories, is like enabling a conversation. It is a clear progression of information between a customer and a business. The customer inquires, and the business responds. The customer asks, and the business answers.

Triggered automated Emails, based on customer actions, are the basis of allowing the customer to dictate the speed of the conversation and the content of the conversation.

Rather than a "batch and blast" Email that will hit everyone with the same message, imagine a one-to-one, personalized approach that responds specifically to a customer's history of interests, purchases, and responses.

It shows that you listen.

ASK FOR THE SALE

THE PRESENTATION OF YOUR CONVERSION

HERE IS A CASE STUDY from a major brand who hired me to analyze their website:

1. They attempted to sell directly to customers from their website, but they were only getting a measly .02% sale rate from their online store.

2. An average month brought in over 200,000 visitors to their online store, with an average sale of $400.

3. They were only making around $16,000 (but usually less) in a month from their online efforts.

They had a lot going for them. They had no problem getting people to the website. They had name recognition and were a leader in the industry. Plus, they had rankings, so there were no problems in the search engines. The problem was their website. Why were people not buying?

In this case, it took a third-party observation to uncover a simple issue. Within moments I saw that the call to action to go to the checkout was mysteriously missing. On further investigation, I realized that it wasn't absent. It was just very difficult to find, because the presentation of <u>the call to action was essentially hidden by the design of the page</u>.

The action buttons were made to fit into the overall design of the site. The "Checkout" button was at the bottom of a page, presented as small white text on a very light gray background. There was not enough contrast to find the buttons. They were out of sight, not clearly marked, and nearly invisible, because they blended into the background.

A simple change of creating large, more contrasting call to action buttons, appropriate to the purpose of the page, increased the sales rate of their site to over 3%, which increased their annual website sales to over $2 million. Now they were asking for the sale.

First, You Have to Ask

For most salespeople, getting to the point of asking the customer to make a decision can be a nerve-racking experience. You do not want to offend the customer or lose the sale by asking too early, but sometimes that nervousness becomes inaction, and the customer is never invited to act or decide.

I've had many salespeople guide me around a store. Some will even tell me what they think about a product. Few ask if I'm ready to buy. There just seems to be a hesitancy among us to get out the words, "Are you ready to buy?"

Expert salespeople are the ones that are able to approach that question, and make it seem as natural as the rest of the process. As with any type of practice, once you do it a few times, it gets easier. You learn from your mistakes and improve. You get to the place where you are not afraid to ask, and then your sales increase dramatically.

BIG, BOLD, & OBVIOUS

Online, asking for the sale is certainly easier for the timid salesperson. However, in the mix of the artist, designer, and programmer, the calls to action may be overlooked as just another element of the page. As a business owner or as a marketer, you have to look at each page on the website and ask, "What do I want people to do here?"

If what you want them to do isn't the biggest, boldest, and most obvious thing on the page, then guess what? They won't see it.

Everyone wants to increase sales, leads, subscriptions, and other metrics, but usually, the pages of the site do not reflect that intention. Articles are written and published. Information is presented. Related links are available; but what is our goal?

If you are expecting people to find that link in the menu and go to the contact page, then you'll be waiting forever. Online, there isn't enough time to ask people to "work" that hard to make contact or purchase. What you want them to do must be presented as the primary call to action on the page, and there must be no question as to what it is, why it's there, and what it will do once it is clicked. You don't have time for anything else.

I was in Kentucky attending a conference, and with some of my available free time I planned to see a few local attractions. In doing this, I found a perfect example to illustrate this point.

A local distillery offered tours, and the website was beautiful. I was

> CALL TO ACTION
> WEBSITE
> EVALUATION:
> 1. WHAT MAKES ME MONEY?
> 2. IS IT OBVIOUS?

impressed with its multi-media and the design of the site, but something was missing.

In the next screen capture, you can see the pleasing presentation of the site, but there was no clear call to action in my immediate view. There was a menu, but it didn't look that important. There was some history and additional text, but nothing looked "clickable."

As I scrolled down the page, I finally found what I wanted at the very bottom of the page, in a nice red, easy-to-see call to action. But it was only easy to see if I scrolled down to the bottom of the page - not where EVERYONE would see it, at the top.

If this button is what brings people to your shop, invites them to purchase, or gains a lead, it needs to be the biggest, boldest, and most prominent feature on the page. It should not be tucked away, where it will be overlooked.

We call this concept "above the fold." It is a newspaper term of prominence. The most important information is presented "above the fold" of the newspaper. Lesser information has to be below the fold, as very few look there first, or even look there at all.

This beautiful concept can be applied to any forms and channels of marketing. If you have an app, is it obvious how people should use it? Is it obvious what they should do?

In addition, let's bring this into your social media presence. Can people find where to contact, purchase, or subscribe within your Facebook page or updates? Are you using your social media to tell people what you do? Are you presenting compelling information about it, and providing a means for them to take action?

Pictured above: What is seen "above the fold" in an average browser.

Pictured above: The Call to Action presented at the bottom of the page.

VISIBLY ASK FOR THE SALE

How visible is your ASK? Many times, we look at webpages in a vacuum, especially as they are being designed. Too many times, being "edgy," modern, or following trends takes over as the primary goal. In designing pleasing and fashionable pages, the purpose of those pages tends to be obscured.

In this example, a heat map overlays a long-design webpage. The "hot" areas are the top of the page and the top of "the fold." After the "fold," where the user has to scroll down to see the rest of the page, the engagement drops off significantly - to the point of obscurity. The map shows a smaller level of engagement in the second level of page scroll, but beneath that level, there is next to no interaction, if any.

The point is this: your main call to action MUST be visible and obvious. In sales, if you do not ask the prospect for the sale, you will not get the sale. The salesperson must initiate the ask for commitment. It works in the same way for your website, app, or email update. Whatever you use, <u>you must initiate the sale</u>.

ASK FOR THE SALE, AGAIN

In any sales training, you learn to expect that someone will give "no" for an answer.

However, during any pitch, you expect it, find out the reason, and attempt to overcome it.

Most telemarketers and floor salespeople will be persistent until they have made you say "no" three times. I like to apply this principle to website design.

While I want to give my primary call to action the largest, most prominent placement on the page, I know that not everyone is there to do the same thing. Nor are all visitors in the same mindset. Therefore, I want to provide calls to action that still provide some level of commitment, but are not as significant.

Ask

My concept is to make the most prominent call to action my highest profit-producing action, such as a purchase, booking, lead form, etc.

Ask Again

The second most prominent call to action is something that may not make me money immediately, but will lead to a profit-producing action, such as an inquiry form, lead form, download, store locator, etc.

And Ask Again

The third most prominent call to action is something that may not lead to a profit-producing action, but allows me to build that contact into a potential sale. This is where I make the pitch to subscribe to a newsletter, download a white paper, attend a webinar, or participate in a contest.

The focus in my third attempt is to get a single piece of information: the Email address.

Once I have the Email address, I have a lead that I can work. This person has given me explicit permission to market to them — on my schedule. I can send promotional Emails, news, information — anything that provides them with information they desired by subscribing.

This may not turn into revenue or profit immediately, and it may take time. The advantage is that you have increased your subscriber base. You have added a name that is a potential customer or client, and you are able to provide them with regular updates and information that may cause them to then commit, and perform an action of value.

ELIMINATE DISTRACTIONS

As it is in real life, things can distract your prospect from hearing your pitch or responding to your ask. Online, there is an entire page of content that can further guide your visitor towards the goal, or it can distract them from even seeing your call to action. Fortunately, these distractions can be minimized, and even bent into formats that point towards the goal, rather than distract from it.

The Color Red

One of the most egregious design flaws in a website presentation is the overuse of the color red. It is a visually jarring color and grabs the eyes' attention. Red is also a color that cannot be controlled from one monitor to the next. As a speaker, I can never rely on the projector that is provided to present colors as

I see them on my laptop. Instead, some are very intense, but the majority are washed out and light.

In the same way, red is a very intense color, and will show differently on different displays. Even from one shade of red to another, different color profiles will present it in varying shades, hues, and intensities. You cannot predict how the color red will render outside of your control.

If there are many elements that are colored red on the page, the visitor's eyes will flit from one red element to the next. In eye tracking studies, visitors tend to look at a page in a Z pattern. Starting at the upper left, moving to the right, down to the left, and over to the right. The addition of red causes this pattern to be completely upset. Red demands the attention of the user, and subconsciously, they respond to it.

Why? Red means importance. It means something is critical and demands attention. If you have only one element that is red, then you are pointing the visitor's attention to that one thing. It is a focused presentation. However, if you use red in 5, 6, or even 10 elements on the page (text, headlines, images, design colors, etc.), then you are communicating that everything is important. Logically, nothing is more important than the other, since everything is so important. It is red.

Use this phenomenon to your advantage. Use red sparingly. Use it to guide the user's attention to a specific point. Only use it when something is the most important element on the page - like the thing that makes you money.

Contrast

Our eyes are amazing things. How a visitor gazes at a website has become a science, as there are certain predictable patterns that our brains use to find information. One of the most basic is the concept of contrast.

Naturally, our eyes and brain move to areas of high contrast. They are the most visually interesting and provide the key to important information. When presenting content, paragraphs of text do not present high contrast. In a sense, they are blocks of single color. However, the larger, bolded, black text of a headline will attract the eyes, because of the stark contrast.

White space in design is the concept of creating open spaces, so that contrasting areas stand out more clearly. High contrast text is the easiest to read, so our eyes move to those areas first. High contrast images make an impact in our vision, as they present clear images.

Conversely, low contrast does not attract attention. In fact, it can repel a user's gaze from the page. Early in the usage of the Internet, there didn't seem to be any rules at all in designing webpages. I was amazed at how many websites used blue text on a black background, which was probably the poorest presentation of contrast one could make.

Years later, I still see this happening, in cutting edge designs and online presentations. Menu text is presented as gray on blue, or blue on blue — which results in an obscuring of important navigational elements. Any time there is light gray or even a medium gray text presented on a white background, the contrast is poor. Consequently, visitors will not read the text. Reading on a digital screen provides enough cognitive and visual resistance, so when additional resistance is offered, such is the case with poor contrast, our eyes move past, to find areas or content that is more easily readable.

As with the color red, we can bend this circumstance to our advantage. If something is important, it should follow the rules I outlined above. It must be presented as the biggest, boldest, and most obvious element on the page. Utilizing contrast to present your ask is a critical factor in guiding visitors to the destination they need, and you want.

Clarity

Clarity is the final element that must be addressed. This is the element of using the right words to communicate the correct idea to your visitor. Avoid obfuscating clear calls to action with jargon, jokes, or meaningless buzzwords.

An example of this is the simple change in button labels over the years. From the beginning, when asking a visitor to fill out any type of form, subscription, or transaction, the button to complete the procedure was always labeled "Submit." It was labeled that way because that's how programmers thought. To them, a form, subscription, or an order was submitted.

A few enterprising people started testing different words in these buttons, and replaced the word "Submit" with the word that clarified the exact action taking place: for example, Send, Subscribe, or Buy. As a result, the conversion rates increased, simply by changing the word.

Thus, the science of online testing was born. Granted, there is much more to the story. The lesson was clear: use words that are clear and communicate a specific concept that matches the visitor's intention or need.

BRING IT ALL TOGETHER

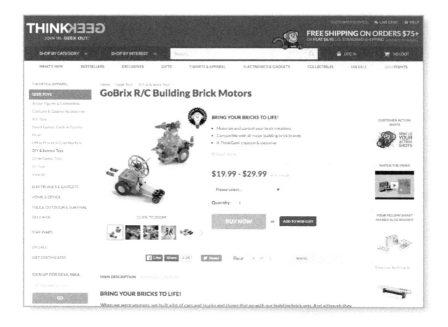

In this example from ThinkGeek.com, we can see all of these elements working in concert to focus the visitor's attention to the goal — the ask.

The product is presented clearly, contrasting against the white background. The name of the product is the second-largest text on the page, and again is contrasting, as large black text in a heavy font against white space. The primary call to action is a large "Buy Now" button. Did you notice that?

Compare the "Buy Now" button with the size of the wish list button on the right. You'll see that the text is different by comparison. BUY NOW is in all caps and is a clear, exciting phrase. ADD TO WISH LIST is in all caps, but is significantly smaller. It is made to look even smaller by using a smaller black button.

Using white text on a black background (or any lighter-colored text against a darker background) makes the text appear even smaller than it is.

In terms of clarity, BUY NOW is a clear call to action. In this presentation, it is unmistakable. In the lower left section of the page, you'll see the secondary call to action — the subscription. The presentation of the secondary call to action does not trump the presentation of the primary call to action, but it is still in a prominent place. It is above the fold in slightly larger text, with an action word in the button.

The primary call to action must always be the most prominent visual element of the page. Anything else minimizes the "ask," and the potential customer may leave out of frustration. Be upfront with your intention and request. Ask for the sale!

PERSISTENCE PAYS OFF

By designing your pages as sales pages, you enable your calls to action to provide different levels of commitment and different benefits to each. While not all visitors are the same, and not all are looking for the same information, the different commitment levels of the calls to action allow them to make a simple choice, based on their level of comfort.

Too many times, I have been part of website development projects, and the focus is on the "look and feel" of the website, in an attempt to be artistically cutting edge. What is left out of the discussion and the design are the very sales elements that directly contribute to the success of the site. It's great if your wonderful new site wins awards, but what if it doesn't make you money? Awards do not replace profits.

People do not go online to be wowed by artistically cutting edge websites. They go online to find information. If they find your site and it has the answers they need for the questions they have, then you may be on the verge of a successful transaction.

If your site is challenging to navigate, presents difficulty in knowing where to get information, and provides little direction, the visitor will not stay. Nor will they be impressed by the cutting edge visual designs and newest programming technology. They want answers — information. Those who provide it will be successful.

I'm not dismissing a good site design or artistic developers. I am warning against those who would sacrifice primary sales elements for artistic design, and those who would focus more on making a statement with the design and programming of the site over the needs of the visitor, or even worse, over the needs of the company. I love beautifully designed websites. I've referenced more than a few in this book, but I've also pointed out where the design overwhelmed a clear call to action — the action that, when performed, makes the company money.

WHAT'S IN IT FOR ME?

CREATE THE VALUE EXCHANGE

THIS IS THE FIRST STEP where the online world carries an advantage over the traditional sales route. In traditional sales, you have to become aware of the needs of the prospect, and draw the information out. After finding the needs, you offer something of importance, either information that is significant to the prospect or guidance.

SUBSCRIBE

Online, the path is much shorter. Unfortunately, what is very simple is usually performed very poorly.

A clear example of this are the many Email subscription forms that I see on websites with the heading "Subscribe for Updates," or countless other variations. The problem is that these do not provide a visitor with enough incentive to give you their Email address.

In an online transaction, we have to view the Email address as one of the most valuable assets of a visitor. When you get that Email address, you are not only getting a new prospect or lead, but you are also receiving permission for future communications and marketing. The Email address is gold!

THE GREATER VALUE

In order to get the visitor's Email address, something of equal or greater value has to be offered. The visitor has to feel as though the information they receive (white paper, discount, freebie, etc.) is of greater value than their Email address. Surrendering one's Email address is giving permission for receiving promotional, marketing, and ongoing communications.

I believe the reason that marketers do not make a better effort to gain the Email address is that they have nothing of value to provide; nor do they see the value of the Email address. "Updates" are not an incentive. I've seen some websites use "Subscribe before it's too late!" But they never answer why it would be too late, or what would be missed.

What is the value of your content? What kind of value will you provide to that lead once you have their Email address? Are you simply going to send them your monthly blast Email? If so, then you certainly do not hold your Email list in high value.

THE LIST

Generations of direct marketers have always put high value on "The List," as it is the primary method of permission-based communications. The best list was the one you developed through your efforts. These are the "hot prospects," because they initiated a conversation to learn more.

Other lists that are bought, sold, and rented may not provide the quality of the list that you generate on your own. The value of your list is unique to you and your business.

LIST BUILDING

Future chapters will present how to market to your list. This chapter is meant to make you think about how you present one of your most valuable calls to action, whether on your website, in your social media, or anywhere you market.

How much attention do you direct to your list-building? Is your Email subscription a campaign or an afterthought? What is the value of gaining a new subscriber, a new prospect, or a new customer?

Gaining those Email addresses is the first step to building your online business. Getting serious about building your list requires that you look at the content or value that you provide and develop a real call to action that presents a clear value exchange.

Ask for It

The first step is to simply look at the pages of your website where you place your subscription offer. Ask yourself these questions:

- **Do you make an offer?**
- **Is it a compelling offer?**
- **Is it clear what the recipient will get?**
- **What promise are you making?**
- **Would you be interested?**
- **What is the goal of the page?**
- **What do you want people to do?**

If you hold your Email list as a valuable asset, then you will want the call to action of a new subscriber to be one of the most prominent and most valuable calls to action on the page.

OVER-OFFER SOMETHING OF VALUE

The problem that I see on most websites is that there is just a simple ask for the Email address, without any promise or benefit described. Let me offer this: "Subscribe for Updates" is not a compelling reason for me to sign up for your Emails.

For someone to give their Email address, you must respect the value of that Email address. It is the right to market to that person. It is the right to send offers, compel action, and intrude into their inbox. Receiving an Email is receiving an invitation to market to someone, so it must be handled with the respect that it deserves.

Offering something of equal or even greater value is the best means of gaining that Email address. Once you have the address, you can utilize it, to turn the lead into a prospect and then a prospect into a sale. First, you need to get that Email.

So, get creative on your offer.

Instead of:

Subscribe for Updates

Get Our Emails in Your Inbox

Stay Up to Date

How about:

Download our FREE 10-Point Guide

Top 5 Sales Techniques to Grow Your List

Get a Free Chapter from ...

The issue is to present an offer to the visitor that is so compelling, so valuable and relevant to their needs, that they not only want the initial offer, but they will also sign up for more.

Value

So, how valuable is an Email address? Jeffrey Rohrs, in his book *Audience: Marketing in the Age of Subscribers, Fans and Followers* (Wiley, 2013), provided this equation to assess the "asset value" of your list. Look at it this way:

If my average customer lifetime value (CLV) is $5,000 ...

CLV= (average spend * transactions per year * average customer length)

... and about 15% of my 10,000 name list are active buyers (I usually define this as active in the past 2 years, but that can vary for different businesses),

Then I have a list asset of $7,500,000.

(10,000 * 15% = 1500) * CLV = Subscriber List Value

Just imagine if I am able to engage even more of 85% of inactive subscribers on my list. I can run a few simple numbers to see the benefit of engaging even just an additional 2% of my list. It could mean an additional 1 million dollars of business potential.

10,000 * 2% = 200 * $5000 = $1,000,000

Running numbers like this is a ballpark estimate, but it sure is fun to see the amazing rate of return by simply engaging your existing list with relevant, personal, and timely offers.

Now, how serious are you about gathering those Email addresses?

ANTICIPATE THE OBJECTION

TURNING OBJECTIONS INTO BENEFITS

THIS HAS TO BE ONE of the most practical, valuable, and deal-saving practices I've ever been taught. It is the difference between a good salesperson and a great salesperson. It is the ability to know the intricacies of the decision-making process so well that one is able to anticipate the customer's reactions throughout the progression.

Not only is this about knowing the sales objections raised by the customer: but the key is also in the anticipation - the planning of your response to any objections. The key factor is in your ability to plan for, respond to, and overcome the objection. And for bonus points, turn the customer's objection into a beneficial selling point. I know some salespeople that have mastered this so well that they can't wait to get the objection, as it presents them with an opportunity to move closer to the deal.

WHAT ARE YOUR CUSTOMER'S OBJECTIONS?

The first step is to know the objections that your customers will raise in the sales process. These can be tracked in a variety of methods — from interviews with your sales staff, reviewing

Emails from prospects, or simply thinking through some of your own experiences and conversations.

You know many of the objections. Maybe it costs too much? That's the big objection that people raise. In fact, it is the main objection. It is the main objection that cannot stand as an obstacle to you. It is the primary objection that you MUST overcome. And we're going to overcome it.

Other objections seem to be tertiary: Time, Delivery, Quality, Terms, Style. We rarely hear those, but they seem to be the areas that can be negotiated or explained. Price is always the objection that tends to stop the conversation. Regardless of how many times price has been raised as an objection, some always seem to be surprised - every time.

Here's what I've learned from over 30 years in sales and marketing: the price is not the real objection.

PERFORMANCE OVERCOMES PRICE

A client of mine shared the results of a survey they conducted among their clients. This was a Net Promoter Score survey, and it was focused on the product. The feedback was somewhat predictable, but it also provided insights as to the value of the client's product.

The feedback could be summed up succinctly in three quotes from three types of customers:

Loyalists: "It's expensive, but it works the best."

Passives: "It's expensive."

Detractors: "It's expensive, and I did not see enough results to justify the cost."

Interestingly, all three customer groups cited the price, even in their "positive" feedback. Price was consistently addressed, regardless of being a Detractor, Passive, or Loyalist. What clued us in to the answer was the language of the Loyalists. When mentioning the price, they always coupled it with a justification. The message was clear that the benefits made the product worth the price.

The Detractors provided the other half of the solution. They tried the product. They were willing to pay the price to find results. However, the results they experienced were not enough to continue the product.

This begged the question: was price the primary obstacle for the Detractors? Of course not! They purchased the product because they were looking for a solution. The mere fact that they had an experience showed the willingness to find a solution, regardless of the price.

Their primary obstacle was a lack of performance. Not price.

The results of this survey and this analysis made a thundering impact on the marketing of the product.

1. The messaging of the product turned from focusing on justifying the price to explaining the performance benefits.

2. Customer stories, case studies, white papers, and interviews were created, as a primary means of communicating quality and performance.

3. In further interviews and research, we found that many of the Detractors had not used the product properly. Because of the improper usage, it hindered the performance and results. A follow-up program was introduced to provide

a step-by-step, programmed text to assist new customers in the application, usage, and results of the product. The guide also provided benchmarks for the first 90 days of the product. It gave the customer the information to look for and identify.

The entirety of the marketing was shifted to focus on the performance angle. And in doing so, overall sales increased by 400%. New customer retention increased by 80%. This was all accomplished by digging deeper into the objection and finding the real motivation.

The trick is not to settle for the objection of price. The price is not the real objection.

VALUE IS THE OBJECTION

This was the lesson taught to me by one of my best bosses (who was also an amazing sales mentor). People say the price is too much. But what they really mean is that they do not see the value.

Think about that for a moment. The price is not the objection; value is.

People clearly do not have any issue at all paying for something when they see the value. We live in a society where people are more than willing to put a purchase on a credit card and pay for it over the next 5 to 10 years, because the value of the product, and having it right now, more than justifies the current and future price they will pay.

Currently, cable and satellite providers are losing customers by the droves. "Cord-cutters," as they are called, are cancelling their cable and satellite packages. Why is this? It's due to the rise of Internet-based movie and television devices, such as AppleTV, AmazonTV, Roku, Hulu, and others. The rise of these devices and access to their libraries of movies and shows on demand has lessened the value of $100 or more on cable and satellite packages. The cord-cutters do not see the value, as they spend less time on cable and more time on-demand. A rise in technology and access in one area has drastically changed the perception of value in another area.

This is where major brands spend millions to affect a buyer's perception of the brand. If the brand is perceived as carrying an intrinsic value, it will justify a higher price. Many brands are much more expensive than their competitive counterparts, but they do not spend time making a price argument or justification. In fact, they tend to ignore it. Those brands focus on your inner satisfaction, your increased quality of life, and the social recognition you will receive as a result of using their brand.

This is where brands have moved themselves beyond the realm of simple products and into that of status symbols. Harley Davidson, Lexus, Apple, Uggs, Nike — just to name a few. The brand is promising more than just the product. There is lifestyle that is part of the product, as the brand says something about you.

When we apply this to our everyday sales and marketing lives, we need to see our proposition from the customer's perspective. Do the benefits we offer provide the value they want? What other factors surrounding the price would make it a more valuable proposition?

TIME, MONEY, QUALITY

The three main objections you will hear are time, money, and quality. Coincidently, they also provide us with the answer to each of those objections.

If the objection is money, overcome that objection with quality and time.

If the objection is quality, overcome the objection with money and time.

If the objection is time, overcome the objection with money and quality.

It seems simple, but it is effective.

First, think about all the infomercials you've ever seen. As they make the pitch and the offer, what do they always say next? "But that's not all!"

> THE PRICE IS NOT THE OBJECTION. THE PERCEPTION OF VALUE IS THE OBJECTION.

...and what happens next? They offer two for the same price - for a limited time. What's happening? They have increased the quality of the offer, by giving 2-for-1. They have also increased the value by decreasing the time that it is available. See how that works?

Infomercials run on a formula, and it works. By making the offer, and then creating additional value with a limited time offer, they are creating a sense of urgency. By offering two-for-one, there is an offer of extra value. These are effective means of creating action in the viewers.

I've hosted too many contracting companies in my home and have been pressured into signing a contract for services on the first appointment. I'm sure that they know that the best chances of getting the contract are on the first call. Allowing the customer to think for a few days will drastically reduce the chances of getting the contract.

So, in order to get your signature on the contract, they keep dropping the price more and more to make it more attractive. But here's the catch - you have to sign, today! The price they offer is only for that appointment, that day. They attempt to overcome your objections by reducing the price and reducing the time that the price is available.

OVERCOME PRICE WITH QUALITY

One of the best examples I have seen of overcoming a price objection was to offer more quality at an even higher price. Discovery Cove provides an excellent example of the technique.

On the Discovery Cove website, there are multiple packages available to select from: the Day Resort with Dolphin Swim Package, the Day Resort Package, and the 2 and Under Package.

You can also add on to the packages to have additional experiences.

In this part of the website, there are special occasion packages for birthdays, engagements, weddings, or other types of occasions. You can also experience being a dolphin trainer for a day in this example, or have a SeaVenture.

Already, beyond the first level of packages, Discovery Cove is offering upgrades that are very attractive offers, to enhance the "standard" experience. For example, the Celebration Package starts at $159, and offers the following:

- a buoy with personalized message delivered by a dolphin,
- Signature Tote Bag,
- photo frame and plush toy,
- and 20% off the Discovery Photo Package.

Of course, that's not all!

The Elite Package takes this to another level with additional features that include:

- a buoy with personalized message delivered by a dolphin,
- Signature Tote Bag,
- photo frame and plush toy,
- A private cabana with
  - A host/hostess
  - seating for up to 6 guests

- private stocked refrigerator
- private locker
- snack and beverage service,
- And the Discovery Photo Package ($229 value).

Wait! There is even more.

As long as you are upgrading, there is always the Ultimate Upgrade. For only $25, you can have unlimited access to all three parks in the area. However, because attendance is limited to 1,300 guests a day, the availability of the Ultimate Upgrade is also limited.

Do you see what just happened there? Each upgrade focused on adding value to your visit. The last upgrade focused on adding value and added the next element — time. You have to hurry in order to get this upgrade, because it is limited and in short supply.

By creating a sense of scarcity with the added dimension of limited time, the value has increased in the mind of the visitor.

Interestingly, all of these additional offers involve assets already owned by the park. The price is simply a cost that they have placed on assets they already own. The cost is presented as an upgrade. The perceived value is what the visitor applies to themselves as they purchase an "experience."

There is an interesting psychology at play in this presentation. There seems to be more space on the website dedicated to upgrading the experience at Discovery Cove than selling it.

By focusing the attention on the greater values available, the question is no longer "how much is it?" but "how much more do you want?" The offer has shifted from selling the initial price to the offer of additional value in options and experiences. Subconsciously, the prospective visitor may only be using the initial price as a launchpad, as it is already established; but greater value is available for only a few dollars more.

This is a tricky sell, but an effective one. Travel does this well. Your vacation mentality tends to be one of rewarding yourself, so you may as well upgrade and make it memorable. Selling additional benefits, recognition, experiences, or even memories are effective means of adding value, without spending time overcoming a price objection.

This is why performance — quality — is the primary weapon to overcome price. If the quality is there, if the performance is there, then the value is there, and the price is simply what needs to be paid to attain that quality.

LOOK FOR THE REAL NEED

WHAT'S THE REAL MOTIVATION?

I'VE KNOWN ABOUT THIS CONCEPT for years, but it took a shopping trip with my teenage daughter bring me face-to-face with its digital application.

We went shopping for shoes. However, the store had dozens of styles. I figured that she would find a pair with the colors she liked and we would be on our way. I couldn't have been more wrong.

Instead, she took out her phone and started taking pictures of the shoes. Then she sat down and started typing on her phone. A few more pictures, more texting. Finally, I asked what she was doing.

"I'm asking my friends what they think."

"How?"

"On Instagram."

And there it was, an entire conversation about her choice of shoes with her friends. And this was what I learned. My daughter was not buying shoes for herself. She was looking for a pair of shoes that her friends liked and approved of. She was looking for real-time influence, which would determine the shoes she purchased.

Did she need shoes? Yes.

Did she buy shoes? Yes.

What was the real motivating factor that purposed the shoes she bought? Peer Acceptance.

And there it was. The motivation behind the expressed need. She expressed a need for shoes, but her motivation was not nearly as simple as finding a pair of shoes that fit comfortably and were in the style she liked. They also had to pass the teen-age-girl-friend test. Wow.

But this is not uncommon. There are always underlying factors to almost every purchase we make, and social acceptance is not just a 15-year-old girl phenomenon. I see adults do it every day.

THE TRUE MOTIVATION

The motivation is what drives us to pick between brands, as the brand says something about us. We want to express the right personality, so we choose Apple instead of Dell. As a salesperson, we know people need our product, but what drives the decision? This is where asking the right questions becomes critical to the understanding of the customer. The more you know about the customer and what is important to them, the better you'll find the real motivation beneath the surface.

Customers provide significant amounts of clues in conversation, so in sales it is important to simply listen and tap into those clues. Online, we have to do a significant amount of research and thought to determine what those clues may be.

This research is done by examining the types of people that are interested in your product or service and considering their goals:

What are they trying to accomplish?

What is their payoff for that accomplishment?

What will satisfaction produce?

What additional benefits may they experience?

Beyond the product, what deeper feeling or emotions may be involved?

At this point, we are getting into the psychology of the visitor/customer, and attempting to think beyond the initial accomplishment of the product. We need to think from the customer's standpoint of deeper emotional needs.

MASLOW'S HIERARCHY OF NEEDS

In 1943, Abraham Maslow published a paper titled "The Theory of Human Motivation." In this paper, he proposed the Hierarchy of Needs. It presented a step-by-step priority of human needs. The needs at the bottom of the hierarchy must be fulfilled before needs at the top of the hierarchy. When the base-level needs are absent, higher needs are unimportant.

The base of the needs hierarchy contains essential physiological needs that we all share and must have met: Breathing, Food, Water, Sleep. Nothing is as important as breathing when one can't breathe. At the top of the pyramid is self-actualization. Self-Actualization is the need for creativity, spontaneity, morality, and problem solving, things that we can pursue when all other needs are satisfied.

This is an important concept to build into your sales presentations. In looking for the real need behind the expressed need, Maslow's Hierarchy is the place to start.

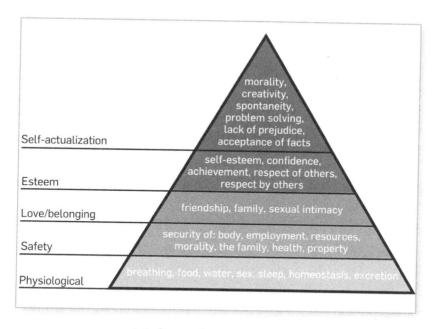

Maslow's Hierarchy Of Needs

This chart shows why my daughter is using technology to gain her friend's real-time feedback on a clothing purchase: Esteem from Others is a more basic need than Self-Actualization.

In a business to business context, this is important to know. When someone is making a decision to purchase your product or use your service, their reputation is now on the line. Their fear of making a wrong decision is powerful: more powerful than mere facts. Making a wrong decision, losing one's reputation, or worse, losing one's job, is a more powerful motivation factor than the logical presentation of facts and supporting information. Self-Actualization, at the top of the hierarchy, is what allows for a logical assessment of facts. Security and employment is at the bottom of the hierarchy, just above breathing and eating.

This may explain why you lost that contract or that sale, even when everything made sense and looked great to the customer. At the last moment, keeping things safe and exactly the same was their priority.

IDENTIFYING DEEPER NEEDS

This brings us to the online context. How can we find these deeper needs when we cannot probe with questions, or listen to the customer? Part of this is your own research and discovery process, but here are some examples to get your creative thinking in gear:

USBCELL

USBCell offers rechargeable USB batteries. I like the idea. In order to recharge your AA batteries, simply plug them into your USB port!

Now this is a good invention, and the presentation could focus on the innovation and need for carrying USB-rechargeable batteries with you. Maybe those that travel understand the need for batteries in cameras, computer accessories, headphones, or other electronics. If that's the marketing plan you choose, you would not be faulted for it, as it presents a logical application of the technology.

However, as we look at the Maslow's Hierarchy of Needs, the intellectual acceptance of facts is at the top of the pyramid. Is there a need that can be identified that is deeper? More basic? One that will create more of a sense of urgency, or purpose?

USBCell does just this in their presentation. The website focuses on ecology and the environment. The headline reads "Eco batteries save money & planet." This is not a large leap to make. If a searcher is looking for rechargeable batteries, then it is a safe assumption that they have some level of eco-responsibility. Buying rechargeable batteries keeps regular batteries out of the landfills, and is therefore more responsible. USBCell takes this to the next level of environmental responsibility. You are not simply filling a need to power your camera or wireless mouse; you are saving the environment!

The website also presents environmental benefits and recycling advice! There is even a humorous animation of cute little bunnies being poisoned by toxic battery waste and becoming mutants.

> HAVE YOU EVER FELT LIKE ADS OR ADVERTISERS ARE FOLLOWING YOU ONLINE?

All of this points the visitor further down the hierarchy of needs:

Esteem: Acceptance from others by being a good citizen of the earth, being socially responsible

Safety: Removing toxic chemicals from the landfills, security of your family and future generations

Physiological: Toxic mutant bunnies — need I say more?

By presenting a persuasive message that reaches down into safety and security, USBCell becomes more than just a battery. It becomes a statement and a socially responsible action, not just a purchase.

Colonial Williamsburg

Colonial Williamsburg was a wonderful vacation to take with my family. We enjoyed learning about our history and seeing how people lived in Colonial America in the 18th century. While there, I was struck with the amount of educational products and opportunities available. There was also a significant amount of historical research being performed by local universities.

The website effectively communicated this idea of education as the prime persuasive factor. This is not just a vacation you will experience at Colonial Williamsburg, but an educational, historical experience. As a parent, you are providing both fun and education. Everyone is learning while being entertained. And we all want smart kids, right? What's better than having a vacation that makes the kids smarter?

Interestingly, the Colonial Williamsburg website focuses the content on a distinctly educational presentation. In the Education section, there are links to educational resources for all ages.

This content includes publications, online games, music, photographs, research, classroom guides, teacher training, podcasts, and vodcasts.

The experience of visiting not only provided a great experience for our family, but during the next school year, my kids were able to go back to the Colonial Williamsburg website for school projects, ideas, and information. From basic information to history fairs to research papers spanning all grades, the website was a wealth of information.

The experience, plus the addition of the rich historical content available, provided a resource unlike any other. By being at Williamsburg, and then referencing it later that school year in a project, it gave us a unique perspective throughout the school project, and an experience to pull from in presenting the information. It was an experience that enabled us as a family to benefit for many months to come.

The website reflects that in the presentation as a destination guide, and also as an educational resource. By presenting a largely educational opportunity, as a family holiday it reaches into the Love/Belonging needs that a family provides, and not just the self-actualization of a school project.

Fisher-Price

The last example, and probably my favorite, is from Fisher-Price. You may know them as the toy company. Many of my toys as a child were Fisher-Price toys, so I was very familiar with the brand. However, if you go to the website today, you may be surprised at what you'll find.

The content is not about selling toys.

The content on the site is more about the psychology of play, and understanding how your child will grow and develop. It is a parenting website. In fact, there is a lot of marketing content that directs you to create an account and subscribe to the age-appropriate development guide.

Starting before birth, parents can sign up and receive regular updates about their child's development stages and how they will act, play, and grow. Included in these guides are examples of the types of play in which the child will engage. At the end of the guides are toys that will help this kind of developmental play.

But before selling toys, Fisher-Price focuses on a deeper need; a much deeper need. This is the need to be a good parent, a caring parent. Fisher-Price isn't selling toys. They are selling assurance that I am a good, caring parent who buys toys that will enhance my child's growth and development. I will play with them the correct way, I will inform myself about their development stages, and I will watch for the important factors.

In fact, the site is more about me and my self-perception as a parent than it is about the child. Strangely enough, it is that affirmation of being a good parent that really seems to drive the motivation. Of course I want my child to grow, develop, be smarter, stronger, and well-adjusted. I want them to get good grades, get scholarships, go to a good school, and get a good job. Somehow I can help them accomplish that if I buy the right toy that helps their little brain to grow.

It's not about toys. According to the needs hierarchy, it goes all the way down to safety. Safety of my family, my child, and their future. It also rises into the sense of Love & Belonging: the idea that I am going to care for this child by not just getting any toy, but only the right toy.

It also speaks to our esteem. We can praise ourselves, saying that we are investing in a child's future by attending to the development guide, and having the right toys that will stimulate development. We know that this expression of love for a child is also esteem for any parent, grandparent, or relative. This crosses multiple needs, and is a powerful draw beyond a simple plastic toy.

FIND THE NEEDS

Here is where you ask the same questions about your service, product, or business. Besides the direct benefit of purchasing from you, look behind the need to find a psychological reason for purchasing.

A good way to start practicing this approach is to watch commercials and keep notes on what is being sold, and the tactic being used to sell it. You may be surprised at how many products are linked to psychological satisfaction rather than a direct appreciation of the product. You'll most likely find that the psychological benefits stated have very little to do with the product, and are more focused on safety, security, attractiveness, quality of life, and acceptance.

Go back to Maslow's Hierarchy of needs and look where your current marketing or sales message ranks. What message or appeal can increase the emotional weight of your message?

Start by answering these questions:

1. What problem are your customers trying to solve?

2. What are the emotional/psychological benefits to solving this problem?

3. How can your message identify and appeal to those emotional/psychological benefits?

Follow-up on Intent

Retargeting: Reminders for the Undecided

THE AVERAGE WEBSITE CONVERSION RATE is somewhere between 2% and 5%. That means that, potentially, 98 out of 100 visitors are not going to convert on the first visit.

The truth is, the vast majority of visitors to your website will go unnoticed, unknown, and possibly undecided in making contact or working with you, your company, or your products. That is a significantly large number. However, the upside to this number is that you still have the potential for follow-up.

Following up on undecided visitors is a bit tricky, but it can be done well. Some are too pushy and eliminate themselves, similar to advertisers following up after an initial contact. Others will be able to reach you, provide good information to help with your decision, and respect your time. How can you walk that fine line and still convert the sale or the lead?

Retargeting.

Have you ever felt like certain ads

> HAVE YOU EVER FELT LIKE ADS OR ADVERTISERS ARE FOLLOWING YOU ONLINE?

have been following you around? Maybe you visited a website and added a product to a shopping cart, but then left the site. Yet somehow that website and that product are following you around! Sometimes, you may have never visited a website, but the ad is still there, everywhere you go.

The quick answer is yes. Those ads are following you.

A LITTLE TECHNICAL BACKGROUND

Every time you visit a website, a small file is downloaded into your browser. It is similar to you bookmarking a website, or adding it to favorites, just in reverse. The website is "bookmarking" you. This is so the website can more accurately count who is coming to their website, when, how many times, and what pages you view.

This file is called a "cookie," as most people know them. Over time, when you return to that website, it will check to see if you have any cookies from a previous visit, and also put new ones in your browser to track each session that you engage in on the website.

These cookies allow the website owner to know if someone views products, adds them to a cart, or browses content. But if the visitor leaves the website without purchasing or completing a purchase, the cookie file also allows the company to position advertising directly in front of that visitor.

Just as a salesperson knows that you are interested in a product, so they continue to provide follow-up information, this cookie tracking process allows the company to advertise their ads in front of you, reminding you to come back and complete the process. Of course some advertisers overdo it. They come on much too strong and turn people off - just like salespeople can easily do, and overpressure a customer. Usually the customer simply makes an excuse and leaves.

However, this is not so with ad technology. The advertiser can determine the parameters of how much exposure they want, what ads to show, and how aggressive they want to be. Some are better than others in this regard, as they know that overexposure can lead to negative feelings on the part of the consumer.

Targeting the Message to the Prospect

Now, here is where this advertising technology really excels. It is most effective when targeting a near-personalized message based on the behavior of the visitor. By creating a scenario-based approach, and crafting a campaign that matches the intent of the visitor, retargeting campaigns have shown significant returns.

In advertiser tests and campaign responses, the trends are consistent. If shown a brand-based ad, people will respond, but not as much as seeing ads that contain the product they viewed while on the site. The more personal the retargeted ad, the better performance it will generate with customers. By showing them the product or information that they viewed, the more they will pay attention and respond.

In addition, advertisers can add additional layers of targeting, based on visitor behaviors, pages viewed, and time-sensitive ad strategies. The actual ad displayed is only part of the overall retargeting campaign. Advertisers can show ads based on the product you added to the shopping cart, the product category or type, or the content that was viewed by the visitor.

Based on the buying cycle, there may be a short time window to target a message to an interested consumer. An automotive buyer may make a decision within a few weeks, whereas someone looking for golf equipment may be making a decision sometime over the next 48 hours. Advertisers can adjust the how much they are willing to spend in order to maximize their exposure to interested consumers over a specific timeframe. For example, an advertiser may set a budget of $5 per impression to reach an interested targeted visitor within 24 hours of visiting the advertiser website. After the first 24 hours, the budget can be adjusted down to $3.75 per impression, as the primary interest period may have lapsed.

DEVELOP TARGETED SCENARIOS

The most interesting retargeting campaign I worked on utilized an existing campaign, running on LinkedIn. The LinkedIn campaign was already targeted to B2B professionals that fit a certain criteria, based on demographics and job titles.

Typically LinkedIn campaigns do well in gaining click throughs (CTR - ClickThru rate: the amount of people that click an ad, divided by the amount of ad impressions). However, those same campaigns regularly have a lesser conversion rate. B2B audiences are typically more familiar with ads in certain industries and receive many targeted campaigns, so they are less likely to convert based on their familiarity.

A retargeting campaign was developed based on gaining those visitors that clicked on the ad, but did not register on the landing page (about 99% of respondents).

The first level of the campaign was targeted at those that clicked through the ad and only viewed the landing page.

This received the lowest budget, and produced less than a 2% conversion rate.

The second level of the campaign targeted visitors who clicked on the ad, viewed the landing page, and viewed 3-5 pages of the website. This group had a retargeted conversion rate of 4%.

The third level of the campaign targeted visitors this clicked through, viewed the landing page, viewed more than 3 pages of the website, and viewed at least 1 video on the website. This retargeting campaign was more focused, and the messaging was more specifically based on the content viewed. Visitors in this category had a conversion rate of more than 10%.

The key is to focus the follow-up on the interest level and motivation of the potential customer. Aggressive campaigns that overwhelm will cause prospects to avoid ongoing contact. Generic messaging or impersonal information does not provide relevant information, other than a brand advertisement. Sometimes it may be enough to bring a consumer back into engagement with the website; sometimes it may require a higher level of communication and relevance.

IT'S ALL IN THE FOLLOW-UP

In the current marketplace of digital marketing, I wouldn't do search engine optimization or paid search marketing without running a retargeting campaign, to capture the unknown visitors that each of these channels will generate.

This gets to the heart of sales and follow-up. The vast majority of salespeople will only follow up with a prospect 2 times (Sirius Decisions). 80% of sales require 5 follow-up calls after the initial meeting, but 44% of salespeople give up after 1 attempt (The Marketing Donut).

This is why online retargeting is so successful. A person who is shown retargeting ad is 70% more likely to convert on that website. Follow-up is essential to the decision-making process. Online and Offline!

Follow-up after the Sale

Email Welcome Series

One of the more interesting psychological phenomenon sur-rounding sales is the concept of post-purchase regret, or "buy-er's remorse." Buyer's remorse is a common emotion after a sig-nificant purchase. We invest in a major product, and it costs us, either in terms of a hefty loan or a significant amount of money, and we wonder if we made the right decision.

Interestingly, this sense of remorse is quickly removed when the decision to make the purchase is reinforced soon after the sale. This is why you will receive a call from a dealer about 1 to 2 days after you drive that car off their lot. They know that buyer's remorse hits you about that time. So, their reassurance, coupled with you restating the reasons for your decision, helps to allevi-ate any remorse. It will never be as strong as you feel it in those first few days. Afterwards, the rationalizations have been made, and you forge ahead.

For a B2B buyer, changing from a long-time provider or tak-ing a chance on a smaller company will inevitably produce these same feelings of remorse:

Should I have stayed with the same company?

The big, established company was a safe bet. Am I taking too much of a chance?

No one ever got fired for selecting Provider A, even though they are bigger and much more expensive - will it cost me more in the long run?

Questions like these are natural, and part of the purchase process. This is also the time when a smart company acts quickly to communicate value, stability, and rewards. In a recent study, B2B buyers responded that follow-up, education, and information post-purchase is very important.

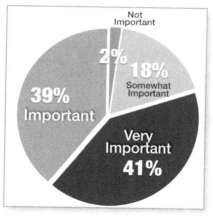

What is the importance of receiving Ongoing Content After Making a Purchase? (US B2B Technology Decision Makers)

Source: Eccolo Media B2B Technology Content Survey Report

A full 80% of decision makers responded that receiving follow-up was important. However, 41% of decision makers also want more than just follow-up; they want ongoing educational and thoughtful leadership content! They want to know how other industry experts are using the product to get the most out of it.

To some salespeople, this is one of the most critical steps in the process. Even though it is post-purchase, it is the experience of the follow-up that cements the decision process of the buyer, and also develops a long-term relationship.

The decision to purchase is most likely an emotional one, yet propped up with research and facts. Therefore, the follow-up must reassure the buyer that they made a logical decision, based on their research and data. In addition, it must allow the buyer to express their reasons for the purchase. Nothing you say will be as persuasive as their own rationalization!

> WELCOME SERIES EMAIL CAMPAIGNS AVERAGE 8X THE CLICK-THROUGH RATE AND 5X THE REVENUE COMPARED TO OTHER EMAIL CAMPAIGNS.

The result makes them feel good, as they once again "feel" the benefits of the purchase. The follow-up language must be couched in both logical and emotional terms to satisfy the basis of remorse.

These next questions are the typical types of remorse. As you can see, they are focused around both logic and emotion, but also on the perception of others. This also provides the framework for your follow-up.

Did I spend too much?

Did I make the right decision?

Will my colleagues (spouse, boss) agree with my decision in the long run?

In today's modern marketing, one of the best methods of follow-up is the Welcome Series Email. As a means of follow-up, it provides touch points at critical times throughout the follow-up process.

A Welcome Series Email kicks off after the acquisition of a new Email address or customer account. This is an automated feature of most Email Service Providers. You can pre-write a series of messages that will introduce your new subscriber to your business, product, or content. It is usually a low-profile sales tool, and brings the new contact up to speed as to what your business is all about.

This can include links to older articles, resources, and information that they may not have seen in their discovery process. Really, when you think about it, you are serving up a PR campaign to a new user, and showcasing the best you have!

After a few Emails that help to build that relationship between you and your new contact, you can make a more practical pitch. Maybe to upsell, cross-sell, upgrade, or increase services —whichever works for your business.

The point of the welcome series is that it is a programmed, automated method of introducing your business to new subscribers or customers, and helping them get to know your business better. The result is that your customers are happier by receiving helpful information, obtaining support for their decision, and building their relationship with the provider. Once you build it, it can run indefinitely until you change it, but EVERY new contact receives the series, which builds additional trust and exposure.

Ultimately, the data backs up this type of relationship building. Companies that utilize Welcome Series Emails to communicate to new contacts show that those Emails generate 5x the revenue of other types of Email campaigns. Open Rates and click-through rates of Welcome Series Emails show that people are open and willing to engage with these types of Emails, because the relationship is new and they are excited to receive more information.

Don't waste this opportunity! On the following page is an example of how one company developed a series of Emails for their new customers.

Prezi is a cloud-based presentation software. After signing up for a monthly subscription to use an online version of the software, the subscriber receives a series of scheduled communications. The Emails present Prezi and the benefits of the purchase the same way as the sales process, yet described in educational "how-to" language.

EMAIL 1: PURCHASE +0 DAYS

The Prezi initial welcome Email is focused on the "how to" aspect of getting started using the software. The Email is titled: *Welcome to Prezi: A Getting Started Guide.*

The Email outlines **three easy ways to get started**:

1. Start from a template,
2. Import an older presentation,
3. Or start from scratch.

This is simply presented, and links to the respective landing page for each start. The landing pages are not for sales, but for post-sale education!

In many purchases of software, the critical part is engaging the buyer early in the process. If the engagement is never reached, the buyer cancels his subscription, and revenue is lost.

Similar to many other business relationships, if the buyer sees no value, there will not be an ongoing relationship. Establishing the value of the product after the purchase is just as critical as before the sale.

EMAIL 2: PURCHASE +7 DAYS

Now, I'm not sure if this was the regularly scheduled Email, or if I received this because I had not yet used the program. Either way, it was specific and targeted to get me into the program.

The first email provided 3 ways to get started. This email was even simpler – a video. Go watch the video, and see how easy it is to get started!

Video is a powerful engagement tool, especially for post-sales education. Seeing HOW it is to be used can often make or break ongoing business.

EMAIL 3: PURCHASE +14 DAYS

This is why I love this example. The two prior Emails were focused on getting me started in the product. Now that I had begun using the product, I got an Email for a free trial of the paid desktop version.

This is an excellent use of the programmed Email, as it educates, educates again, and then asks for another commitment: an upsell, a "hook."

This is an excellent template to follow, as

ongoing communication enables the customer to know that the company is in contact with them. The vendor is not far away and silent, but active — informing and educating.

As a customer becomes more active and engaged, more messages can be developed, to grow and invite them to take another step in the process. It could be an upgrade, a review, or a recommendation.

If you were in touch with your customers this often, and providing value in every communication, how easy do you think it would be to ask the customer to deepen the relationship with you and your company?

When you get a new customer or a lead, this is the time when their interest is at the highest level of excitement and engagement. This is the time for you to guide them, seeing early wins and measurable results. The more you guide the customer, the more valuable the experience will be.

Engaging Emails help them to get more out of the product, so why wouldn't you ask them to do something that is an upgrade, up-sell, or recommendation? It sure beats a cold call to a customer, asking them to upgrade or increase their budget, when there has been no communication since their initial decision!

EMAIL 4: PURCHASE +60

After a little over a month of using the product, the "shininess" starts to wear off. If it does not become a regular tool in the business workflow, then it will not be used consistently. Using a new product, service, or tool must be done consistently, if it is to be incorporated into our regular work routine. If not, it will most likely sit on the side, paid for, underused, and possibly forgotten.

Sooner or later, someone will wonder why they are paying for something they don't use, and the subscription or service will be cancelled. Worse yet, a competitor may have made a more compelling offer, but may not have the same comparable features. In this age, it may have nothing to do with who has a better product, but what information the customer ultimately retains.

This is a good time to get back in front of the customer and remind them of alternate reasons for their decision. In this case, Prezi showcases a product benefit that may not be obvious to the customer - it is a multitasking tool, and can be used in other ways!

The Email highlights templates to generate ideas for the customer. Prezi presents itself as another tool in the arsenal - increasing its value and relevance.

EMAIL 5: PURCHASE +120

The final Email in this series was perfect.

A questionnaire. With one question. THE Question.

You may have seen it or been asked it before. It is based on a simple premise, and the implications are foundational to a company and their customer relationships.

Based on the book *The Ultimate Question* (Reichheld, F. 2006 Harvard Business School Press), this question and the resulting rating provides a measurement score of the attitude and perception of your customers. This is the NPS - Net Promoter Score.

If a customer rates the likelihood of referring the company to a colleague or friend 9 or 10, then they love the product/company. They are a Promoter.

If a customer rates the likelihood of referring the company to a colleague or friend a 7 or 8, then there is something holding them back. They like the company, but don't want to be seen "holding hands." There is something preventing a long-term commitment. However, they aren't negative toward the company. They are a Passive.

If a customer rates the likelihood of referring the company to a colleague or friend between a 0 and 6, then they do not like the company or the product. Generally, people tend to rate things higher (as people tend to be nice, not negative in surveys), but there is a problem. A major problem, and they can usually cite the specific issue that results in this rating. They are a Detractor.

Based on these ratings, a company can learn a lot about how they are perceived and how to address issues with the product, the service, or the company. It is the most fundamental feedback a company can receive - the importance of a referral.

QUESTIONNAIRES AND FEEDBACK

I love this example from Prezi, as they maintain a level of communication by educating me on how to get more out of the product, thereby making it a better tool in my workflow.

In the last Email, the survey, I am now a participant in the process. By asking for my feedback, my opinion, and my rating, I am now a participant in the company and the ongoing improvement of the product. My perception of Prezi is that they take steps to educate people and ask for their opinions, and then use the feedback to improve the product. Even more, my investment may increase in value, as I provide valuable information to them in return.

A WORD ABOUT PROMOTERS

There is an entire chapter on referrals, but I need to address this here. Since I covered the NPS and the importance of feedback, it is certainly appropriate to explore this concept a bit more.

One of my goals in an NPS survey is to find my promoters, but even more so to find out who they are. I want to know as much as possible about my promoters and how they promote. Are they active on social media? Are they well-known in the industry? Sometimes we need to approach our marketing problems out of the digital "box," and go back to analog thinking.

I was surprised that there were not more opportunities to provide explicit information back to the company. For a product like this, I would certainly be interested as to:

- Who is using it?
- How many presentations do they give a year?
- To what kind of audiences?
- To how many people?
- Professional Speakers/Trainers?
- Corporate/Educational presentations?

Why? In order to find out who my power users and influencers might be. Someone who uses the software in public will be a critical part of the word-of-mouth growth of the company. Knowing who they are would be a valuable key in the ongoing customer advocacy and marketing of the company.

I think you see where I'm going with this, but let's keep that for the next chapter....

FOLLOW-UP AFTER THE SALE

How critical is the follow-up in handling buyer's remorse? A recent study by Inbox Group showed that a Welcome Series Email campaign averages 4x the open rate, 8x the click-through rate, and 5x the revenue, compared to other Email campaigns.

Why? Because alongside buyer's remorse is also excitement. Excitement at a new provider, at taking a chance on a smaller, more agile company, a chance to get noticed for making a forward-thinking decision. A chance to get better. And you have to help your prospects get there.

A new buyer is an excited buyer. Feeding customers the information they need at the right times keeps them hungry and excited, which also creates advocacy and referrals. It creates loyalty through a customer knowing that this company communicates well and often, and maybe "reads my mind." A welcome series prolongs the honeymoon and leverages the excitement of the customer, and the openness to follow-up communications.

Companies that recognize the buyer's risk, address the remorse, and educate them to get the most out of the product will not only increase the long-term relationship with the buyer, but also increase their bottom line revenue as well.

Know Your Best Customers

Loyalists Produce Loyalists

O NE OF MY BEST EXPERIENCES with a client was a true collaborative experience. The client had performed a Net Promoter Score analysis of their target audience. In addition, they developed a clear psychographic profile of the audience, and their perceptions of the product. I worked with them to implement this into a marketing presentation that would resonate with their audience.

Besides asking the simple question of "would you recommend this product to a colleague or a friend," we also asked other questions in order to find out more about the attitudes and perceptions of customers, previous customers, and non-customers. One of the questions in the survey asked them where they initially heard about the product. The answers seemed typical until we grouped the responses by Promoter, Passive, and Detractor. That's when we saw something stunning.

The majority of Detractors and Passives learned about the product through traditional advertising channels: event sponsorships, magazine ads, and direct mail.

Loyalists overwhelmingly learned about the product through one channel: **referrals**.

The channel that had no budget, no loyalty program, and no attention was producing the greatest amount of long-term satisfied customers. The channels that cost the most were producing short-term neutral customers. This opened the companies' eyes to the importance of referral and loyalty marketing.

This phenomenon is not uncommon. In fact, I've seen that it tends to be the rule more than the exception:

LOYALISTS BREED LOYALISTS.

When companies focus their attention on the top 20% of their customer base and grow the excitement, the engagement, and the investment in those customers, there is a substantial return. However, it is not a simple engagement. There has to be consistent method and messaging as part of this approach. In my previous story, the messaging and the methodology for sending that message changed to become more consistent across the organization. It doesn't work otherwise.

In other words: give Loyalists a simple message to share.

Combined, these are powerful sharing principles. A consistent message that succinctly communicates the value-benefit proposition of your company, focused on the "best" customer segment, enables your customers to become your best representatives.

After that it is simply human nature. Those most excited about your company will share with their friends. Their friends will tend to be like them - similar demographics, lifestyle, and values. We tend to be friends with people like us, and we share information. Loyalists breed loyalists.

THE POWER OF REFERRALS

In the marketing world, there is constant talk about customer advocacy in social media, making moments matter, and all things surrounding the digitally-based customer conversation. However, I believe that we tend to get wrapped up in all things digital (maybe because it can be measured, or get large budgets), and we tend to forget the most standard of marketing channels – the customer referral.

The experience that people have working with your agency, or experiencing your service or product, is the product! The experiences people have mean more to them than any glossy brochure or Google ranking – and they share it!

The most powerful marketing tool at your disposal is the customer experience. If people like it, they tell others about it. If people have a bad experience, they tell others about it. While campaigns may bring in new visitors, your best chance at referral marketing lies with the customers in your care – right now!

Studies and research consistently show us digital channel comparisons, and only rarely do those comparisons include offline channels. A recent study from Implicit caught my eye, as it presented comparative measurements showing that Customer Referrals, by a large margin, was the #1 conversion channel.

In a survey of nearly 500 clients who also use Salesforce as their CRM system, 3.63% of referral leads from customers and employees resulted in a sale. That doubled the sales rate of leads produced by other channels, such as websites (1.55%) and social media (1.47%).

Even more impressive is a recent study that showed that customers generated by referrals:

_____

- Purchase 20% more per average order/sale value,
- Have a 25% higher lifetime value,
- And are 25% more profitable than customers generated from ANY OTHER SOURCE.

These are numbers that you simply cannot ignore. Every business must have a loyalty and referral program in place in order to produce a steady stream of these high-value customers. This is another type of customer acquisition channel, and it yields an amazing amount of return.

EVERY CUSTOMER IS A SALESPERSON

A visitor's experience is the best advertising campaign and investment. In his book, *Endless Referrals* (McGraw-Hill, 1998), Sales Guru Bob Burg states that ***"Every Customer is a Salesperson....Train them to sell you."***

In any business, this instruction is clear. The experience that a customer has on either end of the spectrum will be shared. Non-experiences tend not to be shared. Those that are memorable, whether good or bad, will be shared. Sometimes they will even be shared digitally.

To encourage a customer to share and be a salesperson of your business, they must consistently experience the best you have to offer – a consistently outstanding experience. This means that all of your employees must be able to act in a way that reinforces the company message, and be able to articulate it in whatever capacity they work.

Marketing is effective in bringing people in the door, but the experiences people have will be the ultimate factor. Those companies that invest in the customer experience are making an investment in marketing.

The problem with training customers is that it starts with you and your company. In order to "train" a customer, your employees must know the purpose of the company, the value of the customer and the message to communicate. Disparate messages and experiences do not "train" a customer. A company must first train its employees to have directed and purposeful interactions with customers toward a specific outcome. Only then will the customer be trained to know the level of service they have received.

I was never more aware of this than when I stayed at the Langham Hotel in Chicago. Now, I have had great hotel experiences where I knew that the staff were focused on the visitors, but the Langham was obviously a step above what I had experienced. I truly felt that I was the most important person in their care when I talked to each employee. Nothing else took their attention: it was fully on me. It made a memorable impression – even on someone who spends a lot of time in hotels.

The problem is that companies do not train their own staff to present a consistent message or experience, so they are not able to "train" a customer to see or explain the company's value to others. Another recent survey found that **nearly 3/4 of companies do not have a "formalized marketing message process for all employees to follow."** Of the companies that did have a formal marketing message process, 60% stated that it was not followed consistently.

Therein lies the key. Each employee must know the message of the company and how it is displayed in customer interactions.

INVEST IN YOUR LOYALISTS

Who is your best customer?

I love asking this question, as I am fascinated by the types of responses I receive. They are never the same. It seems as though people define a "best" customer by many different criteria. I recently asked a friend of mine, who owns a large marketing agency, this question. I immediately followed up with the next question: "Are they your most profitable customer?" She answered no.

When pressed, she offered that her "best" customer was one that had been with her for many years, and they both had built the relationship to a level of significant trust. She had freedom to offer ideas and execute those ideas, as the client trusted her opinion and her work. Another factor that contributed to that judgment of being a "best" customer was that the client also referred business to her. The business that was referred was always "good" business (as she defined it), and the ramp-up time between referral to contract to work was the shortest of any other business channel.

One of the benefits of this, as my friend outlined, is that referral business from this client has been prepped by her customer. The referral always knows what to expect, understands her philosophy of doing business, and relies on the success that she has provided her client.

This makes for a smoother transition in all areas of the client relationship. Pricing is usually not an issue, as the client addressed this in making his referral. Terms are not an issue, as the referral trusts what has been done for the client. The work is proposed and accepted at a faster

> WHAT IS MOST SURPRISING IS THAT MANY TIMES, THE "BEST" CUSTOMER IS USUALLY NOT THE MOST PROFITABLE CUSTOMER.

rate, as the referral has already witnessed the work done for the client and is already willing to move forward, many times without hesitation, to get the same benefits.

For me, my best clients were the longest-term clients, and they were the ones that I enjoyed working with the most. There was personality, trust, and a general enjoyment of the work. It created an atmosphere of collaboration and advancement. Now, I'm not saying that everything was always successful. But the relationship deepened after a few failures and disappointments on both sides. Working through obstacles and building on them created my best client relationship.

RELATIONSHIPS BUILD REFERRALS

In my speaking and consulting business, nearly 90% of all of my business comes from referral channels, which I work similarly to social, traditional, or digital channels.

Working referral channels takes as much work as other channels, as it solely focuses on past and current clients and relationships. Maintaining contact — not pressing for business, but keeping in touch and offering helpful information — goes a long way in keeping long-term relationships.

My referral channel is any client, contact, or relationship where each are segmented based on familiarity. When I send an update, the content of the message is different, based on the past relationship. The deeper the relationship, the more value I provide, and the more familiar the message. Many of the contacts in my list go back more than 20 years, as I learned the value of building a network not just for the immediate benefit, but for long-term professional success.

The value of building a network like this is that you can always go back in the rolodex (or LinkedIn) and find people that may specialize in certain areas and ask for their expertise. Of course, I always look for ways to send business to them. But even more importantly, knowing who to contact, when to contact them, and how to develop that relationship always leads to mutual benefit.

As with any relationship, it cannot be approached with a "What can you do for me?" attitude. If that's how you look at people and prospects, then you will have a miserable time building a network.

Just as important as building that network is thanking those who refer business to you. After 20 years in digital marketing and conference speaking, I still remember two women who referred me as a speaker to their respective organizations. My business and my personal brand grew significantly because of their trust to refer me. I still thank them every time I see them, as I can trace nearly all of my business today back to those two referrals.

How far have you come, and who has been significant in helping you develop your business and your brand? Have you thanked them?

Keep in mind those who have referred you or offered assistance, and always be sure to check in; give them updates and thank them for the time, money, or trust that they invested in you.

BUILDING A REFERRAL CHANNEL

If you are going to take the approach to grow your referrals, you focus on the type of customer you want. This is why I focus on the top 20% of the customer base - I don't want just any customer group. I want the customers that are experiencing the most, that are the happiest, that have invested the most, and that have experienced returns. The ones that can recount their experiences - Loyalists. Those are the ones that will communicate your value in their own words and descriptions.

The key to this is knowing your top 20%. So, what is a top 20% customer? This is for you to define. Is it based on spend, longevity, influence?

To grow your loyalists and top customers, you first have to define what a top customer is.

Typically the formula for measuring your top customers looks like this: *RFS*

R - Recency	How recent was the last transaction?
F - Frequency	How often does this customer purchase?
S- Spend	How much does this customer typically spend?

For every business, this will be different. For a commerce business, you want to look at how often people are buying, how much they spend, and how recently they bought. Then, establish some parameters in each area, such as:

4 transactions per year (Frequency)

Last purchase within 90 days (Recency)

An average order of $200 (Spend)

Apply these (or similar) parameters to your customer files, and you will find a small amount that fit a high threshold. You may find the 80-20 rule in effect, in that 80% of your business comes from 20% of your customers - or something very close to that.

It is the same way in B2B, consulting, or local business. Most of your business comes from a small percentage of your customers. Knowing that percentage and who those customers are will be a critical factor in building your referral channel. These are the customers you need to get to know.

Talk with them. Provide insider information, discounts, rewards - anything that lets them know that you appreciate them. People love to be recognized, and your focus on them will provide that light of recognition. Many times, this leads to an increase of their loyalty, and an increase in their purchasing behavior.

If this group is responsible for a significant percentage of your revenue, then shouldn't you invest in them, and see the greatest return for your investment?

Know what they look like, and then you'll recognize them when you see them. Invest in communicating a consistent and clear message to that group of customers, and watch how they react.

QUALITY OR QUANTITY?

THE CASE FOR MEASUREMENT ANALYTICS

O NLINE MARKETING HAS NO LACK of promises. Just as traditional marketing is full of sales helps, training, and tools to make you a rock-solid powerful selling force overnight, digital marketing makes these promises ten-fold, with basically the same over-promised claims.

At least where traditional sales is focused on techniques, digital marketing makes promises ranging from better search engine rankings and more social media followers to clicks, visits, likes... (you know the rest). But each of those requires a working knowledge of what you are receiving. The word itself does not really imply anything. Ultimately, most of these promises are based on an ignorance of what you really need, but provide something that is "close enough."

In my years in this industry, I am still amazed at the amount of companies that measure success by website visitors, social media followers, search engine rankings, clicks, likes, and page views - all of

MATT'S SALES RULE: BIG NUMBERS LIE

which HAVE NO DIRECT IMPACT on your business. They serve as indicators, but are certainly not the primary measurement of success! They are indirect, and usually serve as a distraction from the vitally important information.

What seems to be rarely measured are those factors that HAVE A DIRECT INFLUENCE on your revenue! Subscribers, Leads, Sales, Conversions - people that take a direct, measurable action toward becoming a customer. These are the things that are rarely measured, but have the most direct impact! When you measure the "bottom line" business measurements, you will know the full story of what is working — and why.

Knowing Your Ratio

One principle that really helped in sales was to think in terms of percentages and ratios to get a sale. If I made 100 contacts, 10 would be leads, 2 would convert into customers, and 0.25 would be a customer for life. This may be different for different businesses, and in different industries. A good salesperson, who has been in the game for a while, probably knows his or her percentages.

Of course, this involved maintaining detailed records of contacts and conversations of individual customers. Old sales traditions revolved around lead cards and the notes kept on them, as they were the key to knowing and increasing your sales.

Those salespeople that measured and maintained this process were the ones that were consistently top producers in their field. Not only could they maintain the ratio: they were always looking at ways to improve it.

But here's the key! By knowing each step of the process and the rate of moving contacts through to become customers, top producers could focus on improving the process. But they did this by identifying a single specific step in the process. They would isolate it, test it, and try new things. After evaluating changes, they would see if there was a good result, and either implement a new process or go back to the old one. They could focus on improving the process in small, clearly identified steps, which would produce clear, measurable results.

IT REQUIRES MEASUREMENT

If you aren't measuring the right things, and measuring consistently, then you have no means of developing a clear process of improvement, based on your feedback. Measurement is critical online and offline for any sales process.

My earliest Internet venture was selling real estate in the mid-90s. By creating websites for commercial properties, I quickly became one of the top producers in my area. One day, I decided to look at all of my numbers and develop my sales ratio, and something very unexpected changed my world.

I was receiving hundreds of leads a month from my websites. I had high rankings in the search engines for all of the critical keywords, and the leads were rolling in. I had created methods for dealing with the sheer volume in order to quickly find the difference between "just looking" and true buyers. **But then I found that none of my sales had come from search engine visitors!**

Ouch!

Search engines were my number one source of visits and leads, by far! How could this be?

I went back to my sales files, looked at all of the customer names, and traced them back to the initial contact. I had saved all of the data from the website and crunched the analytics to find something amazing: all of my sales came from a link on another website - which cost me $25/year for that placement. Talk about a great ROI!

BIG NUMBERS LIE

That day changed all my conceptions of online marketing. It was true - big numbers lie. If all I was doing was measuring leads, I would have continued to invest in search engine optimization - which was not all bad. But finding out that all of my customers came from another source made me reevaluate how to leverage this information to get more customers! Immediately, my system changed. Leads from this source were now treated as high priority, while search engine leads were second-priority - with a new system for follow-up.

It was then that I realized the importance of measuring the entire process, not just the initial numbers. By digging into the numbers as segmented, contextual groups, I was able to find sales gold.

In the same way, digital marketing measurements need to measure the entire process - and the ability to do this today is beyond compare. However, the human factor is critical, and those that understand traditional sales will be able to use it to its full capacity.

Why? Because "traditionalists" understand the importance of notes, lead cards, sales cycles, and experience. Merge these skills with the current digital data available throughout the lead capture and nurturing process, and you have an unstoppable sales team.

MEASURING THE FUNNEL

In sales, you learn very quickly that making 100 contacts is very different depending on where you are. There are opportunities that tend to produce better contacts than others. Business cards in a fishbowl at a trade show tend to produce very low-quality contacts and leads. That'll kill your ratio. Getting that referral - that brings a smile to anyone's face - as the chances of closing quickly are high.

Knowing that not all contacts and leads are the same, we need to take this approach to our digital marketing, with the intent of measuring each channel. Some channels consistently produce contacts and customers more willing to commit than others. Measuring those channels and how customers behave differently among them will provide greater understanding of how to adapt your message to the channel, and build proper expectations.

In addition, we also need to realize that the Internet customer is most likely using multiple devices and channels. How the customer discovered your online store may not be the channel through which they interact and ultimately purchase. Customer behavior is becoming almost as unique as each customer, and better methods of tracking leads and visitors are required for effective decision-making.

ADDING CONTEXT

What is the difference between a searcher who initially finds my site in the search engines, and a visitor who initially finds my site from a Twitter link? Do you know which one has the greater chance of becoming a high-value customer? It is a question of context. By adding context, it informs my channel strategy, and creates a repeatable, predictable process. Context enables you to answer the question of likelihood by creating those scenarios of visitor to customer ratio.

In my investigation of context for my real estate website, I found that the "link" leads were all coming from an industry-specific website. The website was a directory of services surrounding the industry, not just a sales directory. The deduction was that these "link" leads were already in the industry, were very familiar with the process and product, and had clear expectations. Conversely, search-based leads were very early in the sales cycle.

That knowledge created a new paradigm of dealing with leads and evaluating them in terms of data. By taking factors associated with the link leads and utilizing them in the evaluation process of "search" leads, the leads could be even further segmented, in terms of quality.

However, over the next few years, new channels emerged very quickly - and changed the online sales conversation to something entirely new: social media.

Social media offered unparalleled opportunities for one-to-one communications and new channels to access new contacts, and every day those opportunities increased! Headlines constantly shouted the success of social media in creating new audiences and business.

And for many, it was true. And for many, it wasn't.

You see, social media works incredibly well, for many types of businesses. Even then, it depends on what type of social media, and what type of business.

But you add it into the funnel and measure it. What I observed from evaluating thousands of businesses was similar to what I had seen years earlier. Big numbers lie.

Facebook, Twitter, Instagram, Pinterest, etc. You name it - fill in the blank for the next big one.

They do a wonderful job of providing exposure. Do it right, and you can attract the attention of thousands of contacts. You can develop leads, get in front of eyeballs, and increase your digital footprint.

But not all provide the same level or quality of lead.

Many marketers are waking up to the realization that their social media efforts are doing "something," but they don't know what.

Smart marketers track the process, and see which channels provide the best leads - and not only that: they are also able to track the best quality leads, which turn into high quality customers, which provide the highest lifetime value.

WHICH SOCIAL MEDIA?

I'm not arrogant enough to tell you what social media to use. That's not my call. I don't know your business, your industry, your product, your uniqueness, or your customers, so how could anyone be so presumptuous as to tell you what you "have to" do?

The key is to evaluate your audience, and know what resonates with them. Where are they, what do they respond to?

And measure it.

For me? I have found that Twitter gives a good exposure to new articles and news that I've published. I find that Email provides the best source of ongoing and loyalty-based business - consistently. My best Email subscribers come from personal contact.

I've developed my system based completely on measurement and data feedback. And it provides freedom.

More specifically, the freedom to say "no."

Only those companies that know why they are successful and back it up with data are free to say "no." They know what works and why - and don't feel pressure to invest heavily in something unproven or new. If they do, they know exactly how much ROI they will be taking away from their current sales ratio.

Digitally, marketing analytics are now re-creating the lead card and the sales ratio. By measuring visits from different sources and channels, and the behavior of those visits, leads are now measured in terms of quality.

...and it will change your world.

CLARITY IN PRESENTATION

MATCH YOUR MESSAGE TO YOUR STRATEGY

WHICH SOCIAL MEDIA DO I USE? How much time should I put into it?

How will I know if I am successful?

These three questions define nearly every question I receive from business owners about social media. It seems to be one of the most mysterious and baffling marketing activities, and it is frustrating to owners, managers, and marketers alike.

Social media has somehow become divorced from traditional marketing thought and practice. For some reason, people assume that because it is social media, all of the old marketing wisdom either does not apply, or that social media is its own unique entity. It's not. If it is about communicating with people, then traditional marketing techniques will always apply.

Unfortunately, social media is then approached outside of traditional marketing structure. People hear the latest tactics at a conference, or hear how someone "went viral," and then attempt to duplicate it without knowing any of the strategy, failures, or context of the campaign. The result of this is a marketplace of tools and tactics, but very few know what they are doing.

There are plenty of pundits telling us that we "have to" use these tools, along with their suggested tactics. The problem is that the pundits do not know your business.

With all of the emphasis on the media, there is an astonishing lack of emphasis on strategy. In multiple surveys, marketers consistently claim that strategy is their primary problem.

Not budget.

Not tactics.

Strategy.

START WITH STRATEGY

A lack of strategy manifests itself as marketers citing additional problems, such as: a lack of training, a lack of understanding, and a lack of knowing what to measure, as obstacles to running.

So what we have here is a problem of not knowing WHAT to do, HOW to do it, WHY it's being done, and WHERE to get the right measurements. Does that about sum it up?

How has social media marketing developed as this marketing channel that everyone is using, but nobody knows how to use it? I find that many people are more than willing; but they don't understand it, and do not know how, or what to do. Yet they continue. And expect something to happen.

But that seems to be the inherent promise of social media that trips us up. Simply the nature of "being" on social media gives one the expectation of sudden success. Maybe a viral video, maybe a super celebrity giving an endorsement, or maybe sudden success from some strange corner of the globe. It seems that the measurement of success is placed on the maybe, rather than marketing skill and strategy. Otherwise, people would stop doing what they are doing, and take the time to get it right.

The problem with continuing with "doing what you are doing" without a clear strategy is that you are now laboring under an assumed mindset, and fearful of change. The assumed mindset is that you are doing this to expect some kind of return, but not sure how it will happen. You are taking action, but not sure of the results of that action. Strategy is the middle step that is left behind.

Defining a strategy in your marketing, regardless of the channel or technology, is the backbone, the heart, and the oxygen of any campaign. Without strategy, there is no clear objective, no clear purpose, and no clear message.

Face facts. Without strategy, you're dead. All your activity is simply attempting to resuscitate a corpse.

Strategy is clarity, and clarity is necessary to communicate with people, especially in this age of distraction. People spend mere seconds evaluating webpages: not reading them, but evaluating them. Their social feeds receive even less attention. You have but moments of fleeting glances to communicate your message. So, how will you compete?

The first step is developing a clear strategy. A strategy starts by defining your business, not the tactics that you will use.

Answer these three questions:

Who Are You?

Who is your Audience?

What is Your Message?

It may seem simple, but clarity is found in the simplicity of your approach. If you cannot answer these questions with less than a sentence, then you have very little clarity in your marketing. The longer your answer, or the more words being used — chances are you are adding too much information. If you keep using the word "and" because you do not want to leave anything out, then you've said too much.

WHO ARE YOU?

It starts with how you position your company and yourself to the market. This isn't just social media; this is basic marketing. But we have to go back to basics and start over in social media, as too many people just want to jump in, without taking the time to create success.

What does your company stand for in the market? What makes you unique or different? What makes you stand out? Even more to the point, how do you benefit me?

In simple terms, we call this the USP — Unique Sales Proposition. There are many companies that do what you do, so why should I use you?

WHO IS YOUR AUDIENCE?

Let's get one thing straight. Your audience is not "everybody." Your audience is not "the world."

There is an intended audience for your brand, and you must define it. This point of clarity is missing in so many marketing plans. You can tell because the message is rarely consistent - if there is a message.

If you are trying to be all things to all people, then you are saying nothing to nobody. People on social media are looking for information that is about them, their needs, their interests, and their world. Anything else is just a distraction.

To reach the right people for your business, you have to define the right people. The clearer you define that audience, the better you will be able to fashion a message that meets their needs. The broader your message, the less relevant it will be.

In most cases, the tighter the target, the better the approach. By restricting yourself to a smaller group, you can actually be better, clearer, and more consistent, by focusing your efforts on a segment rather than the whole.

You cannot create a message or strategy without a clearly defined audience. The audience will determine the type of message and the need to which you will appeal. A good message will allow you to modify as needed, depending upon the group you approach. This is mainly because the right audience will identify with your message, because of the way they interpret it.

Defining your audience is also critical in understanding how to approach them on social media. By knowing your audience, you will also be able to study how they use social media, which channels they prefer, and why. What's more - you'll be able to see that audiences do not restrict themselves to specific social media channels, but that they use each channel differently, for different purposes.

Age groups, demographics, geo-graphics, job descriptions, and life stages all affect how people use social channels. Studying your target audience will provide significant insight into guiding your strategy in the tactical realm. Knowing where to make your marketing a priority, and how to utilize additional channels in order to maintain a consistent presence in the right place at the right time, will add to your campaign.

WHAT IS YOUR MESSAGE?

Back in the old days of sales, we talked about the "elevator pitch." In 30 seconds, you had to be able to introduce yourself, your business, and your benefit to a prospect. However, in today's market, no one has 30 seconds to spare.

I now call it the "Twitter pitch." Can you tell me who you are, and my benefit to being a customer of your business, in 140 characters or less? No? Then you've lost me.

The only way you can be concise and grab someone's attention is to refine your introduction, your pitch, and your value, into a simple sound bite. Once you have their attention, then you can say more, elaborate more, and sell more. But you have to have their attention first.

Your message cannot be just about your company; it has to be about the customer's benefit. Anything else is not worth their time. Positioning your experience and awards? How does that benefit me? I need to have a tangible benefit spelled out in clear terms before I take notice. That's the social media mentality.

The best messages are very short, memorable ones that provide a significant customer benefit. They do not need to be explicitly stated in your marketing, but think of it as the "measuring stick" for all that you will say. All of your social marketing communication must align with this message before you hit "Post"; otherwise you are not providing clarity in your marketing. You will be going off-topic and off-message, and distracting from your own brand.

The "measuring stick" message is how you want to be known, even in the marketplace. Your communications must align at all times and reinforce that message. In my agency, our "measuring stick" message was simple: 'We teach our clients how to make more money.'

CLARITY IN STRATEGY

As an example, here is how it worked:

Message: "We teach our clients how to make more money."

1. This means that social media interactions are going to be educational.

2. The focus is on clients and their success.

3. In order to make "more money," the focus is on data analysis, and wisdom in making the right decisions and recommendations.

4. It meant that we had to know and communicate the HOW and the WHY.

This provided the framework for social media interactions. The strategy statement was defined as:

> We will not just "do" for our clients, but teach them by providing information (the WHAT) and insight (the HOW) to make better decisions (the WHY).

As a result, the social media campaign was developed to communicate these essential elements, in all of the communications. All posts, updates, contests, feedback, images, and announcements had to align with that strategic message. If a message was not educational and did not meet the criteria, then it was not made.

Without this type of exercise within your company, you will not have a consistent message to take to the market. Your entire marketing (not just social media) will be inconsistent and reactionary to events, rather than proactive and intentional. As a result, your marketing interactions are much more difficult to plan, and nearly impossible to measure.

Align your marketing with this simple plan, and your marketing will transform. Not just your social media or digital marketing, but online and offline marketing will transform too, as you now have a clear, concise, and understandable message to bring to the market. You will even see your face-to-face interactions change dramatically, as you will have confidence in your marketing statement, customer benefits, and presentation.

Strategy changes everything.

STRATEGY: APPLIED

Once you have a strategy defined, it is a short step to evaluate the different types of social media, and see which are more favorable than others in communicating your message. Obviously while some types of media are more visual, others are suited to immediacy of information. Some require long-term investment, but provide long-term ROI.

THE POWER OF SEGMENTATION

PRESENT THE RIGHT MESSAGE TO THE RIGHT AUDIENCE

IN THE PREVIOUS CHAPTER, I described content in terms of measurement. The more context that you add to a particular action, behavior, or channel source, the more you will be able to explore and understand. At its heart, this is segmentation.

Segmentation is the principle that not all people are the same, act the same, or want the same things. Recognizing this fact should change your approach in new customer acquisition, customer management & retention, loyalty, and promotions. Not everyone will respond the same way, and not all will need the same information. Attempting to send the same message to everyone will result in no one listening.

A recent study from Custoria showed that customers who had the highest lifetime value to a retailer came from search. Customers who had a negative lifetime value came from Twitter. How could the source of the customer affect the lifetime value?

The answer is simple. It all has to do with the motivation of the customer.

SOURCE DETERMINES MOTIVATION

Performing a search on a search engine implies that there is a problem of enough significance that it motivates the prospective customer to proactively search for answers. They find the solutions they need and eventually become customers. I believe that the process of searching for answers and finding them creates a level of loyalty to the company that was most visible and satisfactory in meeting those needs.

Conversely, Twitter is a passive approach to gaining an audience, because of the nuance of the channel. People can go to Twitter to find specific information, and some do, but Twitter is not a search engine. One can only find other Twitter users who may recommend, or brands posting promotions. Typically, people are on Twitter to receive updates and news, which are passive activities. As a result, visitors who come from Twitter are much less engaged with the content, and much less invested in finding an answer. It is a task of curiosity rather than a focused and timely need.

Because of these two different channel sources, one can see how a search would provide a longer-lasting higher value customer, whereas Twitter produces less engaged, short-term customers. This is not to say that they couldn't be grown into good customers, but from the very onset of the relationship, they were not as intent on finding a solution as a search-based visitor.

The study shows us that different channels are used for different tasks in the daily life of a consumer. Some of those channels are much more suited to a specific campaign than others, as each are used for different purposes, and people view advertising differently on each channel.

BUILD SEGMENTS BY ASKING QUESTIONS

This is a first pass at segmentation, to give you an idea of how your sales and marketing benefit from asking questions that define the context of the customer.

Questions such as:

Where did they come from?

What did they see?

What did they do?

How much was it worth?

These are questions that force more questions. A question as simple as "Where did they come from?" will lead to more questions:

Where did they come from?

Social Media? Which kind? What post/update/video?

Organic Search? What keyword?

Paid Search? What keyword? Which ad group?

Link? From what website? What is the average performance of that inbound link?

Direct? Was this from another promotion? Can we attribute another source?

Email? What campaign? Which link? Which offer?

This is segmentation: finding the motivational factor of how someone found your website, and then applying context in the form of measurement. After determining source, you move on to determining behavior: what did they see (initially)? and what did they do?

Based on these questions, you can begin to derive behavior models and conversion rates, based on your inbound visitors.

You can find attributable factors that provide insight as to how the initial visitor touch affects the rest of the process.

Focus on Value

By adding the last factor: how much was it worth? You bring in the final attribute - **revenue.** By applying revenue to the equation, you provide clear insight into which campaigns, channels, and messages are performing. Not just in terms of clicks and engagement, but in terms of value to your business.

This enables you to find valuable segments within your own marketing, and by knowing this information, you are better suited for making decisions that will increase your profitability.

I've seen more than enough businesses make decisions based on opinions and external factors, only to cut the budget from their most profitable segments. The net effect of this type of decision-making can be devastating. Some businesses never recover, and will never know why they failed. Making across-the-board budget cuts neglects potential profitable marketing campaigns.

But those who know:

What works,

Why it works,

And how to make it work better

are the ones that will rise above being budget-driven. By segmenting and measuring those segments, they are able to find the goldmine in their own customer database.

Better Acquisition from Segmentation

What is most exciting about studying your segments is the

knowledge gained and applied throughout your business. A better understanding of your customers provides better ways of communicating with them (and better conversations).

Two customers may want my product, but for two very different reasons. I must understand those reasons and be able to speak to both. To be effective in my sales, I also need to identify those reasons as soon as possible. Examining customer segments enables this recognition and the development of skills, questions, and sales methodology to approach customers.

It starts by defining the needs of the customer. In the chapter Find the Real Need, we explored the *Need Behind the Need*: the real motivating factors that customers have beyond the product.

Here is where you start, by developing needs-based segmentation.

What is it that your customers need?

List practical needs that your business offers:

List emotional/psychological needs that the customer needs to satisfy:

This isn't psychological mumbo-jumbo. It's effective. No matter how ridiculous it may seem, we are all attempting to meet some level of need.

Something as simple as a green, well-manicured lawn has a great deal of value in the social acceptance of neighbors, or self-esteem from the pride of home ownership. There is an emotional basis to nearly every decision we make.

Identify those needs, and then group them into categories. Do you see similar attributes? Or are they stand-alone segments?

In the Business-to-Business world, I typically find that there are customers who want to do all of their own investigation, and by the time they have contacted a company, they are 80% down the sales funnel. They are ready to commit, and complimenting them on their hard work of research and resulting decisions will appease their value of esteem, which will make the final commitment easier.

Conversely, there are others who contact companies at the earliest stages and want hand-holding throughout the process. Even though all of the information is contained in PDFs, videos, and the website, you will still be asked to explain the very same information. They need to hear it for themselves, as they are stressed out by the responsibility of picking a vendor. They do not want to make a bad decision. Hearing the information and receiving a presentation are part of the due process. They do not want to be accused of making a hasty or incorrect decision, so all aspects of the process will be drawn out and compared. This type of prospect needs additional support, extra affirmation, and time. Most salespeople will withdraw after some time, as they are tired of the hand-holding, but not realizing the true need of the prospect.

The key is to group these types of needs and behaviors into similar categories. Then, find questions that will enable you to identify the segment as soon as possible. In the previous example, a question such as: "Do you value your own research more than talking to a sales rep?" will provide significant light as to how to segment the prospect. Knowing the answer will let you know if you should provide space or attend to them closely.

From my years in the travel industry, I've learned that if someone uses an alarm clock on vacation, I have a great chance of upselling them tours and activities. From asking a single question of a customer, "Do you use an alarm clock on vacation?" I learn a great deal about their personality. They see vacations as activities, not as rest. They are there to see new things, do new things, and experience the destination.

Personally, I want to be left alone at the beach/pool, and read a book. Refill my drink regularly and I'm experiencing an ideal vacation. I'm in the category that doesn't want up-sells, cross-sells, or activities. If you attempt to do this to me, you may lose the sale, as I will lose patience quickly. When I perceive that you really don't understand my needs, I lose confidence in my choice of salesperson or company, and I will begin search elsewhere to find someone who does understand me.

BEYOND ACQUISITION

The beauty of the application of segmentation is that it doesn't end with acquisition. It is just getting started, and this is where we have the most to learn. Old-fashioned sales techniques based in direct marketing have a corner on segmentation. If you ever want to get the most out of your own customer database, go find a direct marketer.

Direct Marketing is all about segmentation. It was lead nurturing before lead nurturing. Based on demographic factors, you received marketing. Based on your response to that marketing, you received more targeted marketing. Marketers studied demographic and psychographic factors and based their pitch on those factors, and the underlying needs associated with the segment.

Even today, Direct Marketing is thriving, especially when paired with Digital Marketing, as we can couple demographic and psychographic information with online behavior: sites visited, searches performed, accounts created, and purchases. Put all of that information together and we have a completely new level of targeting available in today's market: individual targeting.

Your own CRM (Customer Relationship Management) software provides a potential goldmine of data, just waiting to be discovered. Find your most valuable customers ("A" customers) as a segment and look at the data to see why they are valuable: check common behaviors, products, sources, and preferences.

In examining your "A" customers (Most Profitable Customers), you should find data that directs you to finding common factors. Those common factors will provide a framework to develop a campaign to go after look-a-likes; prospective customers that fit the same data profile of your Most Profitable Customers.

In addition, examining these segments provides a framework to develop your next segment, "B" customers. How do you make "B" customers into "A" customers?

Here are a few ways to find segments in your own data:

Use RFS data (Recency, Frequency, Spend)

Communication Preferences

Content Preferences

Developing customer segments, and understanding how people respond based on the messages you send, will increase your effectiveness — and profitability.

STOP THE BATCH AND BLAST

In Email marketing, sending the same Email to your entire list is called "Batch and Blast." It is also known as "Spray and Pray." This should give you a good idea of the futility and lack of expectations in most Email marketing.

Typically when I audit a company's digital marketing, I find that Email is one of the more profitable channels. Unfortunately, it is usually the most profitable because nothing is being done besides the monthly Email; yet the channel yields a significant amount of revenue. This should clue marketers in to the fact that the channel works and is already profitable, and therefore it can be grown into a profit powerhouse. But how?

Again, Direct Marketers have known this for years. Match the message to the customer based on their preferences. Provide information and content that they want. It seems simple, but it does require a significant amount of work. However, this is where digital marketing provides much faster and easier answers than Direct Marketers ever dreamed.

Through Email marketing, I can see the content that my customers prefer, by measuring the links they click, the purchases, or responses. I can then create segments based on this information. Once the segments are created, I create content for each segment.

For example, if I have a pet store and visitors sign up for my newsletter, I can see what content they viewed on the site. If they view cat products, then I can move them into the cat list. If they view dog products, then I move them into the dog list. Ideally, any subscriber can manage their communication preferences and lists, but by taking this step automatically, I will be sure to provide specific content as expressed by the customer. This increases their positive perception of my company, because I am not wasting their time with cat products on sale when they do not have a cat. A dog person wants dog products and dog information. Segmenting them on the subscription and content level gives them the information they want.

Of course, this is a basic example, but a powerful one. Many retailers, businesses, service providers, and more have implemented this form of communication, with amazing results.

Customer relationships develop faster and are retained longer when communications are relevant. The key is to see the customer relationship as a conversation, and not a series of announcements. Develop segmented messages specific to that group of customers, and watch your sales increase.

THE CUSTOMER LIFECYCLE

Matching the message to the segment involves a study of the customer across their entire lifecycle. Of course, the way that you communicate to a new customer should be different than the way you talk to your most profitable customer. In addition, the way you talk to an "inactive" customer (or an inactive subscriber) had better be different than how you talk to an "active" customer.

Beyond looking at behavioral data or content preferences, you can also enhance your communications by looking at the customer lifecycle. The customer lifecycle is how you identify the stages of interaction and your desired outcome.

Typically, I see a customer lifecycle look like this:

Awareness → Prospect → Customer → Up-sell → Retain → Advocate

It guides the customer process to a desirable pathway and outcome. One fascinating thing here is that many businesses want their customers to become advocates, but there is no formal system of communication in place to create that stage. By identifying it, you've started it. By placing advocacy as part of the lifecycle, you are now forced to reckon with that goal, and work to move your customers toward that goal.

The lifecycle is a practical activity in that it defines the stages of customer development, and shows where your communications are focused. Traditionally, most customer communication is on the Acquisition and Customer stages. There are usually very few campaigns focused on up-selling a customer to a new level or a new service. Even less are campaigns designed to make the customer an advocate. Usually, advocacy ends up in a social media plan, but it fails, due to the lack of a specific or relevant message.

The key in each of these areas is a change or modification of the customer's behavior. We are asking the customer to do something. The more direct and beneficial (to the customer) we make that request, the better the results will be. In addition, a campaign can be developed around each behavioral milestone. Develop the scenario, create the campaign, and measure the results.

DEVELOP THE SCENARIO

A part of marketing important to customer segments and life-cycle stages is the development of scenarios. This is a particular instance in which communication from the company is critical to reaching the customer. This is where using contextual information to develop customer segments is invaluable. The better you know the segments, the better you will be able to create scenarios of better marketing messages.

A maker of sugar substitutes was able to extrapolate data from multiple sources in order to develop a clear understanding of a major customer segment that was previously unknown. It unlocked massive potential in communications, campaigns, and understanding customer needs.

Initially, this company thought that there was a problem with their website, as there was an 80% visitor bounce rate. This meant that 80% of visitors to the site were only viewing one page and leaving without any further interaction. This usually indicates a big problem.

However, upon investigating this bounce rate, I found that it was primarily based on searchers who were looking for conversion tables. They were searching for a conversion of their sugar substitute for real sugar amounts listed in recipes. This was evident from the search phrases appearing in the analytics - phrases such as "How many packets of [substitute] equal 1/3 cup of sugar?" or "How much [substitute] equals 1 tablespoon of sugar?"

What was perceived as a potential disaster of an 80% bounce rate was revealed as the most successful purpose of the website. People were searching for the substitute to sugar conversion information and finding that page from their searches. Of course they left after viewing that page — they didn't need anything else!

But here is where developing the segment and the scenario becomes vitally important. You can't just learn this information and walk away. This was the primary customer use of the website. How can you utilize this information to move customers along the journey?

To first build the segment, a persona was developed of someone who was searching for the substitute conversion table. The search phrases were exact; it was easy to see that a recipe amount was the focus by the amounts searched. This meant that the searcher was following a recipe, and was most likely in the process of cooking.

This implied a number of things:

1. The searcher had the substitute product on hand - they were already a customer.

2. The searcher was in the process of cooking - the search was an interruption.

3. This may not be a regular substitution process, as indicated by the search.

So our persona centered on someone who was baking cookies or cakes, and was in the process of gathering ingredients, or already in middle of the recipe. The search was an immediate response to an immediate problem. The site was not receiving casual browsers, but intent searchers, who needed their information right away in order to get back to work.

So, we know WHAT was working, and WHY. But the key is to know HOW to make it work better and become profitable.

Further research into the website's analytics showed a significant seasonal trend that increased around late November into the end of December. For the United States, that is the holiday season, which is usually marked by lots of cookies. Many families come together at that time of year, simply to bake dozens of cookies for the holidays.

This was also confirmed by researching search engine data to find how people search for sugar-free and sugar substitutes. The data showed the exact same seasonal trend as the business website. We had located our key to the HOW. By providing seasonal information, planned content, and incentives, the company increased their website registrations — all focused around the conversion tables and holiday cooking.

Not only did registrations increase significantly; overall interactions, Email responses, and social media engagement all followed the same trajectory, as this company learned and benefited from discovering their primary market segment and scenario. It was not what they had planned or intended, but the market directed them as to how they wanted their information, and what they found valuable.

LESSONS LEARNED IN CUSTOMER COMMUNICATION

Of course, what made people customers in this case study was not what kept them as customers. Their needs in purchasing a sugar substitute were different than when they were a customer. Therefore, the information needs changed, and had to develop with the customer's journey.

The more detailed the scenario, the better the campaign. As I understand the scenario, I can then plan for different digital media to be utilized, to better reach that customer with the right message at the right time. Not just through Email, but also through display ads, in-app ads, or video ads bought programmatically. They enable me to reach specific customers at critical times.

General ads are forgotten. Personal, relevant ads are seen, and result in vastly superior click-through and conversion rates. These ads are only as powerful as your scenario.

Don't Discount Yourself

Discounts can cost you more than you think

Of all of the lessons I've received from training and from sales mentors, this one has enabled me to maintain profitable businesses, make better deals, and reach stronger agreements. It carries with it a single proposition: do not discount your value.

This carries a number of related applications. When you discount your price, you are telling the prospect that your initial value wasn't justified, as you were willing to decrease the price. As in earlier chapters, most objections about price are objections about the perceived value. If the salesperson drops their price in order to get the sale, they have decreased the value in the mind of the customer.

The best advice I received was to never drop my price without dropping the value. In other words, if the prospect asked for a lower price, I would offer the lower price. However, that lower price meant that certain features or products would not be available. Simply put: no price drop, unless there is a drop in something else. Otherwise, you discount yourself, and no one else is adding any value.

Sometimes an extension added to the timeline for delivery can even be worth a discount. You can even remove a service, or levels of service. But don't just drop your price for nothing in return.

WHAT ARE YOU WORTH?

This was the foundational question that sold me on this strategy. My price is the sum of my learning, experience, expertise, research, and job. It is also the price set by my company, as a value of the product that is being put on the market. To discount the price alone means that I am surrendering some, or all, of these factors, in order to gain a sale. To the customer, the price was not worth that value, and I gave up my experience and knowledge for a lower price.

And what is the reward? For some salespeople you still get a commission. Maybe not as high, maybe a few dollars less, but there is a commission. The business gets revenue, but as any business owner will tell you - revenue is not profit.

Every discount takes money from somewhere. Usually it is from the profit that a business makes. Some profit is easier to discount than other profit, but that is where discounts hit. Just ask any business owner. Every discount not only takes away profitability, but also reduces their paycheck.

A LESSON FROM ABANDONED SHOPPING CARTS

As an agency owner, one of my best experiences was having a seasoned direct sales veteran on my staff. In addition to him, I also had many clients with direct marketing roots. I was always fascinated to hear how segmentation, analytics, and conclusions were reached in the "old days" of database and direct marketing.

My sales veteran taught me a lesson as we were working with a client. The client was running an abandoned shopping cart campaign. You've seen those. If you go to a website and add something to the cart, but do not complete the process, sometimes you get an Email reminding you to complete the purchase, and sometimes ads follow you around to get you back to the site.

Sometimes, you may see those ads or Emails presenting an offer, such as 10% off your order if you go back to your cart and finish your order. That's what people look for. My wife has gotten to the point where she will not complete an order on any website. She will let it sit in the cart for a day or two, to see what offers she will get to finish the purchase.

> ARE YOU TRAINING YOUR CUSTOMERS TO WAIT FOR A DISCOUNT OFFER?

"And that's what we are training people to do," my sales veteran said. "We are training them to wait for the discount, and money drains from the profits." Of course, he was spot on. He was making the case that there are more effective means and messages to get people to finish the purchase without defaulting to the discount. To him, offering a discount first was like throwing money out the window. And he made a great point.

Here's how it breaks down in a test. If I have 200 potential customers abandon their shopping cart on my website, here's what happens if I offer a discount, as opposed to another message. (You may have other results, but I'm sure you'll see the concept.)

100 abandoners	100 abandoners
$50 AOV (Average Order Value)	$50 AOV (Average Order Value)

10% discount offer	Time-sensitive reminder
35 recaptured sales	26 recaptured sales
$1750 in recaptured sales	**$1300 recaptured sales**

Initially, it looks as though the offer resulted in more sales transactions. However, if my profit margin is 30% on these orders, it may change things a bit.

$525 (30% of $1,750)	$390 (30% of $1,300)
- $175 in discounts	- $0 discounts
= **$350 in profits**	= **$390 profits**

This is a very simple test and illustration, but it shows that sometimes when offering discounts, you can actually perform better in conversions and sales, but then perform worse in actual realized profits!

This test showed that the more profitable course of action was to offer reminders, rather than discounts. In fact, when testing reminders, we found that telling people that their incomplete order was only going to be saved for 48 hours was the best performing call to action! (Remember the three objections? Money-Time-Quality? Instead of offering a money discount, we shortened the time that their incomplete transaction would be available.)

This changes the perception of the purpose of the discount. Many times, a simple reminder may be necessary. If additional motivation is needed, then a timing message may be all that's required to increase the chances of conversion.

MAYBE IT'S THE MESSAGE

Ultimately, what I've learned in this respect is that it is all about the message. In dealing with one software company, they only offer a free month of their cloud-based software if the prospect acts within 24 hours. It's a highly successful offer. And again, it comes down to the money-time-quality equation.

Approaching the objection with the right message can entice action, without discounting profitability. Rather than making the discount the go-to action for abandons, incentives, or deal-makers, what if you worked on changing the message?

I know. The easiest thing to do is to offer the discount. Make the offer and it's done.

It's much harder to take the time to think and create a quality offer that creates scarcity, incentive, and value. But then again, it's more profitable. To quote another proverb, "If it was easy, everybody would be doing it."

From Contact to Customer

Nurture a Lead into a Customer

THROUGHOUT THIS BOOK, MY GOAL has been to show how traditional sales training crosses the digital boundary and informs, enhances, and even advances how you can persuade people online. Because the focus is on persuading people, these techniques work all the time; it is simply a matter of applying the techniques to your chosen medium.

Now we see that technology has increased from the Marketing Department to the sales desk. Marketing Automation has emerged as one of the more exciting methods of gaining new customers, developing leads to customers, and nurturing contacts through the sales process. I've been particularly excited to see this technology develop, as it takes many of the mundane tasks of sales and has merged them with marketing and technology to create an efficient, streamlined method of growing new customers.

Perhaps no other technology could benefit from applying sales training as much as marketing automation. The purpose of marketing automation is to gain leads, move those leads to prospects, and move prospects to customers, all through sending timed, automated messages that invite further interaction. Automated Lead Nurturing responds to the preferences and behaviors of the leads, "learns" what they want, and responds accordingly, by moving them from list to list. The list determines the messages they receive.

While these automated methods are efficient and exciting to see, many companies are taking advantage of the technology, but are brunt in their messaging, persuading, and application of nurturing a lead. A sales "touch" is needed in this area, as it automates the analog methods of persuasion and lead nurturing employed for decades, but brings the human touch and experience.

THE PRE-CALL CHECKLIST: GETTING THE LEAD

Back in my B2B sales days, the pre-call checklist was a gathering of data.

- Who am I talking to?
- What is their position?
- What is distinct about their job/company or situation?
- What information can I learn about the company?
- What likely problems do they have?
- What solutions do they have?

These questions could be answered with some basic research. There were many industry publications that enabled salespeople to get a sense of the company they were preparing to approach. The pre-call checklist was to enter into a call as informed as possible about the prospect.

The next step was to qualify the prospect:

- Are they the right person?

From Contact to Customer - Nurture a Lead into a Customer

- Do they have the authority to make a decision?
- Who else needs to be involved?
- Can they afford the solution?

Here's the amazing part. In today's business world, Marketing Automation is enabling a gathering of data that would make an old-school salesperson's head spin. You see, marketing automation is the process of gaining leads through various online sources, by trading something of value for contact information. It doesn't need to be a lot of contact information, just the Email address.

ONCE I HAVE THE EMAIL ADDRESS, I HAVE PERMISSION TO SELL

At this point of gaining the contact, you may simply be using a database, an Email service provider, or a CRM (Customer Relationship Management) system, to record your captured contacts.

Marketing Automation can be part of a mail program or CRM, but it can also be a stand-alone product that offers those types of services as well. Some Marketing Automation systems will even integrate with a web analytics product, and record what leads did on the website, how many times they visited, and what pages they looked at — even as anonymous users! But then the system will also tie those previous anonymous visits together, when that prospect registers as a lead.

And now I have a full picture of the information that prospect viewed on the website. I also know what ultimately persuaded that prospect to give up their name, Email address, and company name.

It may have been a:

138

- Webinar
- White paper
- Research paper
- Survey
- Paid Search Engine Advertising
- Ads on Facebook, Twitter, or LinkedIn
- Retargeting ad based on a previous visit

All of these content marketing sources drive a visitor to register for access to that content. Why is so much information given away for free? It's not. It's meant to get your contact information, which is the price for all of this free information.

Now that I have your contact information, I can send you information that I know is relevant to you, based on the pages you've viewed, content you've downloaded, webinars you've attended or videos you've watched.

I can match your company information up with a data service and know all of the public information about your company. My Marketing Automation program will file your contact information accordingly, knowing the "ideal lead" profile and scoring your company information. I'll also be looking at your title, company size, and revenue, and asking what purchasing authority you have. If you don't give me that first, I won't worry, because I'll ask it again when you want more "free" information.

At this point, Marketing Automation takes on a few different methodologies, all defined by the terminology used. There are different aspects of automation and different levels utilized. It is important to know what you want to implement and what is required to do so.

6 Stages of Marketing Automation

Build Systems and Sales Processes

Level 1: Automated Email Triggers

At its core, marketing automation is about sending timed or triggered messages to a specific group of people. It can be as simple as an automating an abandoned cart Email that is triggered by a known customer leaving the website. Autoresponders, 'Thank You' messages, receipts, Email verification messages, and confirmations are all examples of triggered Email messages that are based on a transaction.

These can be upgraded by developing additional sets of triggers. An ecommerce site may Email you based on simply visiting the website and browsing products. You may get a reminder to reorder a product that you purchase regularly. You may also get Emails based on your birthday, anniversary, or anniversary of becoming a customer with that website.

These types of messages are personal and timely. They are based on customer factors, behavior, and known event dates. Based on this, Email templates can be developed, which are then customized based on the specific user and the set of rules for each trigger.

LEVEL 2: WELCOME SERIES

As covered in the earlier chapter, "Follow Up after the Sale," a Welcome Series is a pre-planned set of Emails that are developed specifically for new subscribers or leads. Once a new Email is placed in the database or Email service provider, it can be designated to receive a series of Emails at timed intervals.

These are effective means of educating new contacts about your company. Since the new contact was looking for information and found something interesting on your website or from your business, they are excited. Communication from your business is highly relevant, and when received in a timely manner, critical to developing a good customer relationship.

A welcome series can be used to educate, provide history or a complete view of your company, or simply recommended content that may already be produced on your website. It can be as simple as my local greenhouse, which gathers Email addresses at the register during check-out, and then follows up with a welcome series about plants and flowers, and advice for the upcoming season.

These series only run one time to the new visitor (hence the name "welcome series"). Once the welcome series Emails have run their course, that visitor does not see them again.

But what do you do with those that have already subscribed? How often are you communicating with them?

LEVEL 3: DRIP CAMPAIGN

On the heels of the Welcome Series is the Drip Campaign. In most Email Service Providers, CRM, or Marketing Automation systems, this is simply a matter of defining a set of Emails to go out at regular intervals.

Based on the previous section's questions, what happens after the Welcome Series? Well, the obvious answer is to create a set of Emails designed to follow-up and move that lead into a consideration phase. From a B2B standpoint, they are still only a contact. Possibly from a B2C perspective, they are a contact (maybe a subscriber), but not a customer.

Drip Campaigns answer the simple question of how to move a contact along the process to become a customer. You use Email, primarily, to send a timed series of pre-planned messages that inform, educate, and invite the contact to learn more about the company, see available products, or gather more information. From my sales training, this is where you ask the prospect if they have enough information to make a decision. Now I can simply serve up a series of informative Emails, with links to additional content and resources, and allow the prospect the freedom to research on their own.

The advantage of a Drip Campaign is that it provides consistent visibility in front of a prospect. Based on the sales cycle of your business, it may determine how often you time your follow-up messages.

The disadvantage of the Drip Campaign is that it is simply a process. It is a rule set in your system that sends messages to anyone that is in the assigned "Prospect" list. Every prospect receives the same Email with the same information.

So how do you remedy this, and become more targeted and personalized?

LEVEL 4: SEGMENTED LISTS

Now is when we really have to start working. As you've

most likely surmised, Marketing Automation requires a lot of pre-planning work in developing these timely messages. As the targeting and effectiveness levels increase, so does the amount of work and consideration in your messaging.

Segmentation is where Sales, Email Marketing, Marketing Automation, and Customer Relations really start to come together for a unified effort to better communicate to the customer's needs.

A Segmented List is based on developing common categories for your customers. For example, if I have a pet products business, then I would ask people which type of pet they have. (Dog, cat, or both). Based on the response, I would assign that contact to the appropriate list. Dog owners will now be put in the "dog" list, and receive communication about dogs and dog products. Subsequently, cat owners will be assigned to the "cats" list, and receive communication about cats. If someone ticks both options, they are then assigned to either both lists, or a specific "dog and cat" list.

This is both the beauty and hard work in Marketing Automation. Customers receiving specific communications based on their content preference? Amazing. Developing pre-planned content on dogs, cats, or both? Ugh, work. However, it is work that pays off. Big time.

My recommendation in creating Segmented Lists for your drip campaigns is to start small. Be conservative, and only develop two primary segments. As you see it working, or find additional opportunities, develop more. Please do not attempt to do it all at one time. Start small, see results, learn, and build on those results.

A word of warning: I've seen too many companies attempt to take on a project of developing 10 segments and 6 drip campaign Emails for each segment. This meant there were 60 Emails total to be pre-planned, written, designed, and scheduled into an automated system. Unfortunately, they never completed the project because there wasn't enough time. Surprise, surprise.

The major key is in the simplicity of giving people the information they want and need. By eliminating what they do not want or haven't opted for, you are able to keep the conversation focused on the customer's expressed interests. Otherwise you are only providing canned company information, and hoping that what you are presenting is still relevant to the prospect.

In sales, this was easy. You simply asked what needs people had. You kept notes on information requested, questions asked, and conversations that brought up specific needs. Based on that feedback, you were sure to only provide information that was pertinent to the conversation. You don't want to "muddy the water" with irrelevant information, or products that just aren't going to advance the relationship.

Take a key from sales and learn how to quickly identify potential segments, and develop communications that are specific to them. You'll find that the feedback and response rates will justify your efforts.

LEVEL 5: LEAD NURTURING

Here's where things start to get really cool, and really scary - scary in the fact that this requires even more work, imagination, and thinking to get this part moving. It is like sales magic, because your prospects are doing all of the work in guiding the sales process for you. Do it right, and you'll know who to contact, when, and how ready they are to make a decision.

Lead Nurturing takes the Drip Campaign to the next level, and "learns" about the prospect. All of the prospect's interactions, content, and behavior are recorded, and used to determine their next level of communications.

Drip Campaigns, while automated, require manual set-up and intervention. A user could update their preferences, which would change their assigned content lists. Lead Nurturing Campaigns, typically run by a CRM or Marketing Automation System, adjust communications on the fly, as they learn about specific prospects.

In a Drip Campaign, the entire series will be sent to the prospect at timed intervals, maybe a week apart. In a Lead Nurturing system, a prospect may come back to the site, download additional information, and look at videos, pages, and content that would put them into different segments. The assignment to different segments would happen automatically, and the system would move that user from one list to another - based on a set of rules.

The basic thing to understand in a Lead Nurturing, environment is the essential programming instruction: "If This, Then That." Rules are defined by creating scenarios of user behavior.

If a prospect **views 2 videos about *x*** (this)

Then add prospect to ***x* list** (that)

Or, as one of my favorite examples:

If prospect **views pricing page** (this)

Then *move* prospect from x list ***to close list*** (that)

This example was one of the greatest examples, as I was personally a prospect for a software vendor. I had been receiving the nurturing Emails, which were getting more and more relevant every week, as the system was tracking my clicks, content, and interests. However, as soon as I visited the pricing page (and left without purchasing), all other Emails stopped, and I immediately received a promotional Email. For the next week, I received a series of Emails designed to get the sale and close me as a customer. After about 10 days, I went back to receiving the regular Emails.

This is a primary example of automating the nurturing process. The system learns about your interests, and can be set to trigger events that move you to additional lists, or put you into a "closing sales" list, based on visiting the pricing page.

What any salesperson wouldn't give for this bit of knowledge! The power is being able to deliver a closing message or a closing offer to a prospect within moments of them expressing interest in making a purchase decision. This is where that human touch and a bit of sales knowledge can really help. That "closing" message has to tug the right strings and make the right offer, and can't be clumsy in the process. Knowing a bit of sales training and persuasive techniques can make this message a highly effective tool.

The basic concept of the Lead Nurturing system is that you set a series of rules, based on the prospect's behavior. Typically, this behavior is seen in pages viewed or interactions on the website, and also in links that have been clicked in Emails. These page views and link clicks help the system to "learn" the prospect's interests, and will move them to new segmented lists or Email series, based on the rules that you define.

LEVEL 6: LEAD SCORING

Yes, all of this tracking goes somewhere. And at this point, we finally get to a part of the Marketing Automation process where the machine does most of the work. Up to now, it's been a process of defining segments, developing communications, and creating scenarios and rules in order to send the right message to the right person.

Lead Scoring is another layer of this process. If you have a system that is tracking the behavior of visitors, prospects, and customers on your website, then it is a simple step to this level. Lead Scoring takes much of the activities of the user and assigns a value based on those actions.

Lead Scoring is made up of two components: Implicit Data and Explicit Data.

Implicit Data:

This data is the passive collection of links clicked, pages viewed, and documents downloaded. It is essentially the non-verbal behavior of the prospect. Actions and sign-ups such as webinars, subscriptions, account creation, surveys, and user management are all tracked and considered implicit data. This is data that is the result of activity.

Explicit Data:

Explicit means that this is data that has been communicated directly to you by the prospect, such as name, Email address, company name, address, and phone number, plus any survey responses, questionnaires, or other data that is pertinent to knowing the prospect. In sales, this was the lead card: the one that recorded all aspects of the lead, their contact and business information, and their expressed interests and needs. The bottom line on Explicit - it is data directly provided to you by the prospect.

Actions (implicit)		Actions (explicit)	
ACTION	**SCORE**	**ACTION**	**SCORE**
Page View	1	Title	12
Subscribe	10	Company Name	8
Click email link	2	Company Size	6
Download WP	4	Company Revenue	10
Register for Webinar	2	Timeline for Purchase	10
Attend Webinar	6	Location	8
Case Study Pages	1.5	Budget	10
View Pricing	4	Purchase/Decision Process	8
Video view	1.5	Organizational Structure	6
Subscribe Podcast	2	Competitors	6
download podcast	2	Products Needed	10
search	1	Current Issues/Problems	9
search co. name	4	Other Vendors	9
search product name	4	Lead Source	6
survey complete	8	Purchase Authority	12
page views/day	1		
page views/week	1		
social share	1.5		
comment	2		

These two data methods work together to provide a full view of the prospect. Information they provide is very valuable; information they view and download provides a context to the stated needs. Ideally, their behavioral interactions with your website and content matches the expressed needs they have provided.

When it comes to scoring, explicit data is weighted more heavily than implicit data. The more a prospects provides to you, the faster their score accumulates. Each action or event is scored according to the value that it provides in qualifying that prospect as a customer. You can score actions differently based on your business.

This doesn't even have to be limited to Business to Business applications. Retailers use this all of the time to find their best customers. Typically, by using a formula of Recency, Frequency and Spend, they are able to identify and segment their high-value customers. Based on that identification, they can send loyalty incentives, invitations, and specialized offers, just to that high-value audience.

THE BENEFITS OF LEAD SCORING

Once I know enough about you, my Marketing Automation Lead Scoring program will let me know that it might be worth a call. The amount of information gathered from our interactions, such as Emails, links you've clicked, webinars you've attended, videos you've watched, and forms you've filled out, will be matched to a defined point threshold. Once it's met, it's time for me to call you.

The conversation won't be strange or awkward, and it certainly won't be a cold call. I'll be looking at a customer record that shows me what content and information you have been reading, downloading, or watching.

Here's the bottom line: we will be able to have an informed conversation about your company's needs.

Marketing Automation and Lead Scoring eliminate the unknown variables of a prospect's interest by recording all of the interactions that happen in the "anonymous" environment of the website. By recording how often a prospect looks at information, searches for more information, and interacts with information (webinars, videos, downloads), a salesperson can see the opportunities for solutions play out in front of them - without ever talking to the prospect.

Once the call is made, my Automation Software and Lead Scoring System will show me the information that has been most important to you. It will provide me with what I need to ask better questions - questions that are more specific to your needs and the information that you've received so far.

It is a more respectful conversion. It is a conversation about the content you've been looking for, and not a pushy salesperson attempting to guess at your needs. It is truly a partnership that has developed, and the conversation can be more focused on meeting the needs at hand, rather than the salesperson attempting to figure out how their solution matches your needs with no information at their disposal.

AUTOMATION PROMISES VERSUS REALITY

Sound like a sales fairytale? For some companies, it is. They have developed systems that engage prospects through automated messaging, pre-written messages, and segmented lists that provide the right message at the right time to the right person. These messages contain links to relevant content, options to help winnow the content selection, and tracking to know what is viewed, clicked on, watched, downloaded, and seen and acted on.

The key to all of this - a successful Marketing Automation and Lead Scoring system - is knowing how to sell to people. To sell effectively, you have to understand the customer's journey from beginning to end, work through different scenarios and anticipate their needs in order to deliver the right offer at the right time. This amount of success comes at a high price: the price of planning, scheduling, developing scenarios, and testing.

Automation doesn't create a process for you to follow, it's the opposite. Marketing Automation automates your sales process.

YOU CAN'T AUTOMATE WHAT YOU DON'T HAVE

I am amazed at the number of businesses that want to implement marketing automation, but do not fully understand what it is. As the subtitle explains for this chapter: you can't Automate what you don't have. If you do not have a process in place, then automation will not create one for you. Or, in computer terms - garbage in, garbage out.

Marketing Automation involves predictable, repeatable patterns of customer actions, which are then automated according to responsive scenarios. It creates a logical "conversation" with the lead, or the customer. It becomes a sales force for your business, as it automatically creates personalized and relevant messages for your audience. If you do not have those scenarios identified, or the responses created, then you cannot automate anything.

At its basic level, automation is highly effective. A good Cart Abandonment Email can recover as much as 64% of abandoned sales, according to WorldPay. This first step into Marketing Automation can yield awesome results. However, it requires the ability to create a persuasive abandonment notification, and incentive to complete the sale.

Marketing Automation excels in

> OFFERING ENGAGING CONTENT IS GREAT FOR GENERATING PROSPECTS. BUT IT'S A WASTED EFFORT WITHOUT FOLLOW-UP, MUTUALLY BENEFICIAL INTERACTION, AND PROPER SEGMENTING.

lead generation and ecommerce business models. It enables a slow approach to building leads, nurturing leads, measuring and scoring leads by activity and engagement, and then developing models for closing leads. By utilizing Marketing Automation, many of the customer conversations and data disclosure steps can be automated and tracked throughout the lead cycle.

However, despite the promises and shininess of the Marketing Automation showroom, the ultimate factor in the effectiveness of any Marketing Automation campaign is the human engine under the hood. Ultimately, humans have to create the correspondence, design the messages, select the best products/presentations, and develop the rules, scenarios, and processes of the system. No machine will do it for you - you are the primary engine and the fuel of the system.

Because of this human factor, it is in the best interest of anyone developing a marketing automation system to understand the basic principles of sales. Sales training teaches you to be a strategic listener. The more you know about the prospect, the more you can position the solution according to their needs. If you do not listen, then you are most likely missing the expressed needs of the prospect. No one wants a salesperson who does not respect them, or does not listen to them.

ASK THE RIGHT QUESTIONS

By learning how to listen and the key concepts of question-asking in order to get the prospect to talk more, one learns how to position the opportunity, based on the prospect's own information. In this way, the prospect sells themselves on the opportunity and the product.

One rule often repeated in sales training is "Whoever talks the most, loses." This is based on the concept of question-asking and strategic listening. The right questions expose more information: the motivation of the prospect, the timing of the decision, the factors involved in the decision, etc. Most salespeople already know and have prepared questions to start the conversation. They know the primary objections in advance and have prepared for them, in order to turn them to their advantage in the conversation.

Automating your marketing is the practice of predicting questions, events and concerns that are typical of a prospect. By strategically writing, presenting, and delivering these concepts to a prospect, and measuring their response, the sales process is transferred online. Those that understand the process and how it can be applied online find a natural fit. Those that adopt Marketing Automation without an understanding of how to apply a sales process will be exposed in their execution. For example:

SCENARIO 1:

Action: Download white paper - referred by a link on Twitter

Result: 3 sales calls (phone messages) in 2 weeks

Diagnosis: No nurturing campaign - straight to sales calls

In this scenario, the initial interaction launched a full phone schedule to act on a possible lead. However, there is no lead nurturing that takes place: only a full-court press to make contact and talk to the prospect.

In this case, the prospect is only interested in some data that they saw referenced in a Twitter link. They may not be at all interested in the company or the product, just the data. In this case, the time and attention of a person used to make these calls may be wasted.

An automation program could add this contact into a relevant, segmented list, and offer more white papers or resources related to the first. Actions could then measured, and a plan for an approach developed, based on the reactions of the prospect.

This example is the equivalent of a trade show attendee browsing your lit rack and looking at a glossy brochure - are they a target for a full-on sales pitch? Not likely, as most booth sales staff might acknowledge that action. Additional questions need to be asked in order to establish a true interest.

Attempting to approach, by phone, a prospect who accessed a single white paper may be too much, too soon. What do you really know about a person or the lead itself to justify the time and effort of that level of follow-up? What kind of close rate might you predict for this type of process? How could you improve it?

Scenario 2:

Action: Pre-webinar call from registration. Attendee is not looking to buy, merely curious about the information advertised in the webinar.

Post-webinar result: Follow-up call asks if webinar attendee is ready to purchase from the demo.

Diagnosis: Sales rep did not record results of the conversation properly, which results in a segment mis-classification, which launches a mis-targeted automated nurturing campaign.

Remember the human element? It moves to the forefront of this situation, as the entire process comes down to the salesperson's accuracy in recording notes and entering them into the system. If it is entered or classified incorrectly, then your automated lead communications and subsequent follow-up will be mis-targeted, and look erroneous.

At the least, the prospect will most likely unsubscribe from future Emails, as they are not relevant to his or her situation. In other words, the automated system works just fine, but the salespeople need to be aware of how an incorrect entry can lose and possibly alienate a prospect.

Scenario 3:

Action: White Paper offer through a third-party list. I responded, registered for access and downloaded the White Paper.

Post-Registration result: Follow-up Emails offer past white papers, studies, and survey results. Eventually, based on my interactions, the company puts me into a specific product list for further engagement. 3 months after registration, a phone call from a sales rep inquires about my activity and business needs based on the content I have viewed. Results in a sale.

Diagnosis: By allowing the prospect (me) to determine the content that was important, and recording the actions, preferences, and behaviors, the company was able to place me in the right content list for specific product communications. The information I received was valuable and applicable to my business, and resulted in my purchasing the product, with a little "push" from the sales rep.

This is the ideal Marketing Automation/Lead Scoring scenario. It is the goal to work towards. However, it also stakes out the amount of groundwork to cover, as it requires pre-written Emails and communications that have specific calls to action, which result in learning about the prospect. The messages have to be presented in such a way that they add or winnow the content needs of the prospect.

In other words, the system has to be in place before anything can be automated.

The sales system.

What's Next?

How do I improve my skills?

THERE ARE MANY RESOURCES IN the sales world: some good, some bad. The trick is to find the good sales books and manuals that will develop your entire skill set as a communicator and marketer.

I would recommend finding a sales training course that focuses on these areas. A good course is one that will teach you to ask the right questions and to properly listen to the response. At its core, sales training is not about learning a slick presentation or "magical" closing phrases; instead it is about asking the right questions that will lead a prospect to making their own decision.

If you are interested in taking a sales training course, I would recommend finding a sales training or sales consultant in your area. I took a course from Sandler Training and was impressed at the content and philosophy of the sales process. Some trainers are better than others, so be sure to ask around, and find the superstars in your area. I have really enjoyed my training and the instructors that I have met over the years.

ARISTOTLE'S RHETORIC

One of the most amazing things that I found in the training was how much the concepts mirrored Aristotle's *Rhetoric*, which I studied in college. It is the book that caused me to fall in love with persuasion, rhetoric, and the means of influencing people. More than 2,000 years later, the same principles are being taught to some of the most powerful CEOs in the world, and the best salespeople around. I still refer to it regularly, and it is well marked-up and highlighted.

Good information is timeless and valuable to learn, and it is ultimately applicable, no matter what the technology.

RECOMMENDATIONS

I also recommend a few books that have been invaluable in my sales and marketing career:

Endless Referrals, Bob Burg (McGraw-Hill, 1999)

Marketing out of Control, Keith Wardell (2007)

Convergence Marketing, Richard Rosen (Wiley, 2009)

Buy-ology, Martin Windstorm (Doubleday, 2008)

Leading with Questions, Michael Marquardt (Jossey-Bass, 2005)

The Sales Bible, Jeffrey H. Gitomer (Morrow, 1994)

How to get Your Point Across in 30 Seconds or Less, Milo O. Frank (Simon and Schuster, 1986)

The Elements of Style, Strunk & White (Macmillan, 1979)

The Sandler Rules, David Sandler & David Mattson (Pegasus Media World, 2009)